What others are saying about *Awaken! Spirit Is Calling:*

I read most of Awaken! *in one sitting. Helena's words were channelled from her guides and angels, who helped her recover from debilitating illness. This book contains powerful truths for each person's journey and the transcriptions of angelic language served me as meditation. Reading parts aloud brought me harmony and hope.*

Sharon Montgomery
author, Your Invisible Bodies: a reference
for children and adults about human energy fields

It has been my privilege to know Helena personally and to encourage her to take Awaken! *to publishing. I wondered for years what secrets angels would share if they happened to tap one on the shoulder. I finally found out. We all owe a big thank you to Helena for acting as a scribe for this heavenly message.*

Agnes LaDon Kirby
script writer and poetess

Helena is a clear and gifted channel on the path of Spiritual Awakening. A seeker of the truth and holistic living. Her book Awaken! *spoke to me of presence and simplicity... life can be effortless if we stay in the NOW!*

Doris Nickel
Calgary, Alberta

I quite enjoyed Helena Kalivoda's book Awaken! *It pulled at my heart strings and brought out a few tears in places. There are many ways to conduct your spiritual path. Ceremony and ritual combined with discipline are well recognized. What Helena's book does is lead you to the process through the heart with the one prerequisite for it all—love. I highly and often recommend* Awaken! *for anyone who wants to start out on the right road in their spiritual journey. May you enjoy this inspired, personable, informative and endearing offering from the heavens.*

S. Roger Joyeux
author, The Story of Light: Path to Enlightenment
and The Story of Light: Through Heaven's Gate

AWAKEN!

Spirit Is Calling

Helena Kalivoda

AWAKEN!
Spirit Is Calling

Copyright ©2008 by Helena Kalivoda
Published by Audrenar Books

ISBN: 978-0-9738544-2-8

    1. Spiritual life. 2. Self-actualization (Psychology) -
        Religious aspects. I. Title.
  BL624.K34 2010   204   C2010-901902-4

The author designed the information to represent her opinion about the subject disclosed. The author obtained the information contained through personal experience and speaks from her perspective and experience.

The author disclaims any liability, loss or risk incurred by individuals who act on the information contained herein.

Editing: Sascha Kalivoda
Photography: Mitchell Kranz
Cover design: Dominique Petersen
Cover art: Pilgrims, original oil painting by Jaroslav Kalivoda

www.awakenbyhelena.ca

Printed in Canada
First printing 2009
Second printing 2010

This book is dedicated to humanity.

Acknowledgements

I extend my heartfelt thanks to all who participated in this project.

To my Universal Brothers and Sisters, as they sometimes call themselves, to my guides, angels, all those I cannot see but hear when I sit down to write. Thank you all for the messages and your trust you have in me. I am very grateful to you and I acknowledge that you supplied the information contained in this book.

A special thank you goes to my family for supporting me during my sickness and in my writing. Further thanks to LaDon and Rita for reviewing my manuscript and contributing their valuable feedback. Above all, I express my gratitude to my beautiful daughter Sascha who patiently worked countless hours, days and weeks editing my growing manuscript. Without her help this book would not be possible.

I thank my husband Jaro for contributing his Pilgrims painting for the cover of my book. To me, the light surrounding the pilgrims in the painting symbolizes my own life journey, the gold and white light representing shifts in realizations, perceptions and beliefs I experienced while writing the book.

Table of Contents

Foreword

Helena contracted food poisoning at the beginning of December 2001, which continued on for several months. She was not prepared for the onslaught of the illness that deprived her of any sustenance and strength. The experience was frightening. She lost a lot of weight and was in constant pain.

During the course of her ill health, Helena decided to write about how she felt. She summoned her declining energies, and started expressing on paper the feelings and emotions that she'd been holding in most of her adult life. Every day she sat down at her computer to type all that which she felt she needed to express in order to facilitate her healing. At the same time, Helena started intercepting the information that we began transmitting to her. Thus this book was born and is now presented to you.

The book contains quotes written in the Language of Light, which is spoken in the angelic realms. This language, of which there are many dialects, is based on light frequencies and has been converted using letters of your alphabet in order to suit your 3-D environment. The Language of Light brings vibrational frequencies that are soothing and healing. We used it to supplement Helena's medication to help her to gain strength and to be able to receive our transmission. We are happy to report that all has worked out, and Helena is on her way to a full recovery.

Through these writings, we seek to awaken those who are not aware of their spiritual nature. We seek to awaken those who have already been feeling unease in their lives and do not understand where it is coming from. This book was also written for those who are already aware of their spiritual origins and would like to receive confirmation. All who will read it are ready to comprehend that this period of time in which they live is the time to open their hearts and examine their ways of conducting their lives.

Seti mu ne o.

Helena's Guides and Teachers,
Helpers on her journey through her
current experience on Earth.

Notes Regarding the Angelic Language:

I received the information presented in this book through what I can at best describe as a voiceless voice. The angelic Language of Light came in syllables that I did not comprehend, nor was it explained to me. I believe that angels, being pure spirits and of light, possess a language of their own. They speak and manifest their thoughts to their own kind. As they are immaterial, they do not speak by words of mouth but through a wordless exchange of ideas.

Throughout the dictations, the voiceless voice guided me when to come, when to take a rest and come back again. It asked me to focus and listen, sometimes through a gentle scolding, sometimes through advice. Occasionally I received healing energies, which brought relief from the pain of my illness and my back pain from prolonged sitting at my computer. I left the material as intact as possible, including remarks directed to me.

Helena Kalivoda, March 2002

*During the crisis do not open the wounds
but seal them with love.*

*During the fight do not lash back
but send love.*

*During the misunderstanding
do not forcefully explain
but say your peace with love.*

Chapter One

And So the Dictation Began

The sickness was taking its toll, and I felt weak early this morning. I sat behind my computer and started typing, expressing my hurts and dissatisfaction. Suddenly, thoughts that did not feel like my own started pouring out. I had a hard time keeping up with what was coming and typed as fast as I could. This is what was said:

Bill yourself a victory! This is the beginning of the book we will dictate to you. Dear Helena, first of all we need to congratulate you on your understanding of the origins of your sickness.

What is this? Who is this? I wondered. The voiceless voice continued:

We also would like to comment on your approach to spreading goodwill and helping others around you to see their way.

Well, yes, I wrote a couple of letters explaining my feelings to my partner, I thought again. And it went on:

Once you broke through this understanding there was nothing that could stop you.

Thank you, I replied in my mind, and they answered:

Be here on time every day, keep up the good work, and we can start.

And so the dictation began.

Almost everyone in this century will be shaken to the core of their being, seeing the results of planting the seeds of the malevolence and evilness of their doing. "Their", as in that of the human race. Greed is prevalent. We can see the decay setting in many walks of your lives. Political corruption, corporate greed, racism, exploitation of minorities, of children and women—the list goes on.

The knowledge that we will impart for all through these writings is invaluable in understanding everybody's role. The responsibility of changing humanity's ways does not lie with leaders alone. The responsibility is not only up to an individual. The responsibility is en masse. The implications are enormous. If you understand the consequences of this, you will start unravelling that which is causing the descent of the human race—separation from your spiritual self.

Once the masses understand this, progress will move from unattainable to attainable. The masses' understanding is that which we are after. You have a saying "If you don't use it, you lose it". In this case we can say, "If you don't get it, you won't survive".

Helena, we understand that you have misgivings about intercepting our transmission, as you are not sure of your understanding of all this. You keep wondering whether it is coming from your own mind or from "above". Rest assured that this is coming to you from the leaders of the Federation of Enlightenment. This Federation is composed of numerous bodies. It has many purposes and its many bodies look after different subjects: peace, enlightenment, schooling, communication of knowledge, and so on. Many of them blend together, and many of them seem the same. We are those who bring through peaceful means knowledge to Earthlings in order for them to come in contact with their spiritual links and to be able to realize their potential—the spiritual identity en masse.

During the course of this writing, there will be others who will contact you. Many subjects of interest will go on from your mind. Some of these are not of the writings intended by us. However, the rule is that all will be of godly origin. Thus, if you make such a point, it is channelled.

Regarding transmitting, you are an open channel. The channelling as of so far has been pure, and we intend to keep it that way. In addition, Helena, make sure before every session that you invoke the purest light and that no other kind of entities or messages are encountered. Further, keep yourself grounded, which is a good precaution to being usurped by others who are not entrenched in the light. Therefore, with this, we need to say that the writings are off to a good start.

Dear Helena, assume a comfortable position and be aware of what you are typing but do not interfere. Keep your mind still.

Yes, I am working on it as much as I can.

Sera mi natu o. Lati pela cosi ta emi no ri luminu et reti solitu.

3

Esperanto it ain't our dear. It is not Sumerian either. It is older than the oldest. It is the finest. Syllables are matched to melodically underline the harmony that is everywhere where love is.

Trus o trist amyna myst deli ta o ma ruti sela vila. Dela mo noti pa aki, leti solita. Tis a me tis ame dela ti mu.

Such is the strength of the spoken word. Such is the strength of the word. The word, the sound, the vibration, echoing godly vibrations. Pouring through the universes, pouring through bodies, through all things. The word, the sound, the vibration. It is the spoken presence of God.

Silu ki pi? Et tu ku? Celi mino u? Deri mani opu la. Es mi na eti la.

These rhymes bring light and love. These rhymes are based on the Light Language. The Light Language is not a way of communicating on your planet. However, many other civilizations use this language, of which there are many variations. It is based on the projection of light coming into your vicinity. Through light, you can ascribe yourself a pretty nifty linguistic phenomenon and will soon be able to communicate with all those who are receiving the language. As not all who receive understand, the next step in your evolution is to comprehend the meaning of the uttered syllables. Once you understand, you will be able to use the language to communicate amongst yourselves.

Tis me ni? Et ti ku? Deri mula oma ti? Selt orea. Elti. Bilu min ao. Mani ku pe ri, esti, esti. Bi si o.

Ist mi nu la. Eki to ra, ase mi nu la me tu li. Esti patu ke si. Esti malu nal, esti, esti.

This is not a way of diagnosing your linguistic abilities. It is showing us how much light there is around and in you.

Deti minu la. Api solita. Deli mul omi, deri okita ma ti. Sela o, sela o.

Dela mu ti sa asi tu. Dela mu ti tusi mu. Seti pa? Oti mu? Dala kataa reoinu. Seti o la mait bel duri akola mu sel dil a meni roti so el tu okilna mit to. Sel tu oki. Delti moti. Seti la seti la. Amen.

Delti ma ku ti. A la omi. Delti lumi na. Oti demi no. Seti mo, seti mo, atu mi no le dila mo. Seti mo. Seti mo.

Your I Am is seeking companionship, is looking into your vocabulary to enlarge the contacts you have. I Am, or I Am that I Am, is your "cosmic" name. It is that part of you that is divine. It is an individualized presence of God for each human on Earth. The above words are not anything you can translate now, but they should give you the feeling of being cared for.

Der re mila otipu. Seti la mino, oka ati okati. De la. De la. Mi notu. Seti moni no. Delati peru kali omeni lati suli patulao pen lamin delai okuli tremole amino qi sela opu, pali no.

Certainly, language is a tool of communication. You may say, "But I do not understand, as this language is not one that I know".

Ce ci la. Tu li mi no? And does it matter? The melodic voices in your heart are not a hindrance. They are commonly called angelic voices. They come through your psyche. Your receptive mind can accost them and transcribe them into the letters of your usage.

Certain alphabets are harder to learn. Certain prepositions do not match. Certain letters are different. But still, the languages have the same origins. Human speech is based on dialects of angelic realms. You, who live on your planet Earth, do not know these dialects anymore, but they used to be common in the past.

Why don't we know these dialects anymore?

Because time changes. You forgot your roots. Your connections were severed. Your links discarded. These times in which you live are about re-establishing the links, as the links to your original self are not something that can be forgotten and left alone forever. However, sometimes a millennium or more can pass before the links are restored.

And this is such a time. This is a time of re-establishing the links. This is the time for re-establishing your past acquaintances. This is the time for you to step out of your earthly shell and soar toward your brothers and sisters who have been waiting for you for millennia. This time is a peculiar time. If you do not miss this time, in these times of upheaval, you will be rewarded as never before possible. You will celebrate your newly awakened joy and pride. You will be rewarded million-fold. You will rejoice and will be rejoined on so many levels that you have never thought possible.

Desti ma no? Oki tu? Reti mina lo? Ati o me? De la tu li. Mena oki no. Tera ti. Peli mo. Asti lu ne lo mi. No ra tu li po li. Seti la seti la. Esti me no? Seti la seti la. Dali mu ti elo ne? Seti la. Seti la.

Dali me no eti. Meno ala tu. Seti la seti la. Este me na mo? Redo ta le oka? Asti me no seti? Dela meno uta. Seti la seti la seti la.

Dasti dasti meno le. Dasti dasti eko mi. Dasti dasti ole to. Dasti dasti mine ke. Dasti dasti emu? Dasti dasti no ne. Dasti

dasti elo ti? Dasti dasti du li no. Muni muni ati le. Muni muni se ti.

Such is the language of gods. Such is the language of angels. The syllables flow and flow, and leave the best feeling in your heart. Your heart sings with these sylla-bles. Your heart is massaged and loved by these syllables. Your heart knows that these syllables are healing. This is the power of the spoken word, of the voices of angels.

Angelic voices sing in harmony. Many choirs of angels sing and embrace the planet. Their vibrations are healing and help support the energetic patterns of Earth. These patterns are misaligned or sometimes broken, and the harmonic overtones of angelic choirs help heal them.

This part of the message was brought to you by the angelic forces that are looking after the abundance on Earth.

This is enough for our introduction. We would like to start a brand new chapter, and for you Helena, this is a brand new chapter of your life as well. We trust that you will be able to bring this information to your contempo-raries. We trust in your abilities to convey all that is brought to you, to your family, friends, and to all those who are interested in finding their true selves, to all those who are interested in moving on in a positive direction.

And that is all. Let us begin.

Chapter Two

Awaken

As the new millennium neared, you exhibited many different excitements and sentiments. Some of you feared the year 2000 and gathered food supplies, water, and other commodities. Others greeted this new millennium with excitement and joy, and with hopes of peace. What happened next, the growth of war industries, terrorism, war in Afghanistan, to list a few, demonstrated that joy and hope alone are not enough to douse the last pockets of evil. Yes, evil is a word we do not often use, but in this connotation we can say that it is a fitting description of that which is now prevalent on your planet—wars and warmongering, preserving the money interests of the magnates, poverty, support of the puppet governments by regimes that hunger for power and control. This all is a way of advancing the old. It is not a case of enlightened societies dealing with unenlightened societies but of the stronger exploiting the weaker.

Visibly shaken citizens of America are forgetting that which was bestowed upon them (reference to September 11, 2001) was in turn bestowed upon their planetary brothers in Afghanistan. Do not fall into a trap of believing that war is a resolver of conflicts. It is not and never will be. Oppression is oppression. Killing is killing. It is that simple. You may ask, "How can you compare the two? America is a free country, whereas in Afghanistan there were and continue to be so many acts of oppression." Perhaps. However, the distinction is not as visible when you understand at our level. Distinction is in the approach. Eye for an eye does not work. You cannot stay in greed, control and hatred of others. You cannot keep on suppressing, exploiting, killing and annihilating others. Natural law is not supported by this approach. Natural law is love, love, love.

The uprooting of evil is the way but the means cannot be evil. You need to change the way you look at the world. War and warmongering are threats to all economy and to the lives of many people. They are threats to the stability of all nations on Earth. The leading quality needs to be the heart way. The governments of the U.S.A and Russia need to converge and work together. The government of China is one of the powers that have a role to play in future global events as well. Because of its size, China can influence the result of the global shift toward a more enlightened society. It is not certain that this influence will come to be true, but the potential is there. China has a long history of being at the forefront of many historical events and inventions. New and unexpected events may arise from this country of the Far East.

Helena, you seem to be fading away. We understand that your illness has taken a big toll on you. Therefore, we can stop right now.

Not yet. Please continue.

Yes. Discussions are reigning regarding the influence of the U.S.A. Are these good guys or not? Neither. All is one, and there is no separation. The forces of Divine are everywhere and in everything. This does not mean that the reality is such that the U.S.A is not cajoling the entire world to dance to its tune.

Ast la mi tu? Del tou o?

The U.S.A. in general harbours an egotistical belief that they are chosen. That they are the best. That they are the strongest. However, their glory will pass into oblivion. Their glory will be surmounted by Mother Nature.

Es tu lamu? Ne ti pu? Do you understand? Helena, these are not your opinions. (*I was just judging all that I have typed so far, as it seemed odd to me here and there.*) You are getting the text from us. It is important that you take yourself out of this. You are not the author of anything. You are not bringing anything. You are merely transcribing. We are transmitting to you, and you are typing. Have no doubt that all you write is from us. If you wish, you can take a break.

> *Thank you. Tell me, why are you dictating this book to me?*

To help you feel more at ease and give you perspective on your life. To calm and help other people who are ready to listen and need help. It is written for you, for you as in humanity. Humanity needs to awaken, needs to move on from the cycle of greed, wars and wickedness. Your link to your divine self has been cut off. Your spiritual connection with your divine self has been severed. You need to reconnect with your divine source. This is the time for you to realize that your spirituality does not depend on any government, organization, ideology, doctrine, or religion, but depends on you. This is the time for the human consciousness to evolve.

Now, enjoy your day and be back. We love you and we cherish you. Amen.

❧ ❧

I took the rest of the afternoon off. I looked forward to coming back and receiving more of the messages, and decided to try again the same evening. The dictation continued:

Si ku ti mali no. Amo ne pirito. Asa ta male ka delini rolima. Ami no vet so ala.

During the years of depression after the 2nd World War, some went on to live a hopeless life. The war brought a lot of desperation as people lost many of their relatives. It also brought happy moments once the war finished. This conflict on a global scale had to play out to show the meaninglessness of racism.

Did it help?

Of course. But the same menace has started to raise its head once again, along with other menaces.

The 2nd World War is not a war you would like to remember, apart from the fact that an even bigger war may be looming right now. Many principal nations' leaders are warmongering people. These leaders need to change.

This is a call to get together and combine for a big overhaul of all leading world governments. Many are needed in the decision-making economic and political positions, who know better than to realize the required changes through a global armed conflict. These individuals need to step forward and become active in strategic government roles to influence the outcome of world events toward the light instead of the dark.

For the next few years, the prevalent theme will be peace, although warmongering will be very visible. We also believe that the dominant trend will be toward a calm, adjusted life of many living in prosperity and peace.

Many?

Many, as this millennium is about peace, about prosperity, about human values of honour and respect, about not being greedy and materialistic.

The Ring of Fire is being activated. The Ring of Fire, a zone of frequent earthquakes and volcanic eruptions that consists of volcanic arcs and oceanic trenches that encircle the Pacific Basin is staying where it has been for millennia; however, hatred and misery are activating its power. Mother Earth will unlock the Ring and use its influence to help peace come into realization, to come into the minds of the people who are ready to understand that peace is the way, not war. That calm is the way, not unrest.

Unrest and war are not what we want you to have on Earth. Peace and calm forever, we wish that upon you. Each day is a step toward peace or not. Each day is a step toward war or not. It is you who will make these choices. It is you, humanity, who needs to decide which is the way. Is it peace or war? The choice is clear. And if not, then strife will come to clarify the choices.

This concludes today's discourse. Namaste and sayo-nara. Amen, and we wish you a nice evening.

Amen. Thank you for coming.

৩৩

I started on time the next morning.

During the times of unrest in the 2nd World War the human psyche underwent a transformation. This was so global and prevalent that it changed humanity's values. Life and the value of a living creature were never more devalued as it was then. This is again rampant in the human psyche and supported by all the violence in movies, TV and through other media. It is spreading through children's books and toys. It is showing up in all aspects of life. It is not too well understood, but what it does is make humanity less valuing of life. Life is taken as replaceable.

Organs, genes are being manipulated, shifted from one life form to another. This disregard and disrespect for the creation of God and Goddess of yours, who are your creators, is so prevalent that less and less concern is shown, and more and more greed governs humanity.

Sit straight Helena.

> *I was crumbling painfully behind the computer monitor as my muscles were weakened from my illness. I could not eat and had not moved too much for several weeks already.*

We need your spine to be straight, as the transmission is not coming through properly.

*Right, I replied. My back hurts down the middle,
between my shoulder blades. Please work it out
of there, and help me with my lower back pain.
Work it out so I can sit straight without hurting
and trying too hard.*

Release your pain. You need to release it. You need to
know that you are fine. It is not us who can help, we are
merely facilitators. Say to yourself: "My pain is gone. I do
not need this pain. I am strong and pain has no room in
my life. I do not need it to remind me of anything. I have
my priorities straight. I know my purpose, and pain, as a
distraction from my path, is not welcome. Pain, would
you leave me? You are not needed anymore. I command
you to leave right now. Keep away, as my body is supple
and is no longer tight and entangled in pain."

Thank you.

Is it gone?

Yes, I feel better.

Good. Let us continue.

You repeat your experiences through various lacera-
tions and war conflicts. The brutal face of humanity is
becoming increasingly brutal. In the name of a country,
in the name of religion. In the name of governing politicians, in the name of industry, in the name of war
machines churned out that must be used—why else
would they exist? All this equals a conflict that must be
resolved.

All need to stop and examine their motives. Why am I
involved in this brutality? Do I believe that this nation is
threatening us? Do I believe that by demolishing their

homes and killing their families, fathers and brothers, I help to have a better life for people in my country? Do I believe that or am I being misled? Do I use my heart or do I succumb to the rhetoric of warmongering governments, generals, arms makers, chemical weapon makers, plane and ship makers—who, of course, can make more and sell more, and build their riches based on the blood of the people killed and maimed by their inventions. Am I that convinced that this is the way to go? Am I convinced that this orgy of killing will lead us to calm and peace? Do I believe this all? Am I afraid to say what I really believe? Do I fear that I will not earn enough to support my family? Do I believe that this is the best for my family and me?

Ask all those questions and more. Ask with your heart and see what it replies. You should not be surprised, because down deep in your heart you already know it. You already sense it. You already were deciding on not participating when the mind came in and said, yes, you will, it is your duty to your country. Is it? Is that what your duty is? Your duty and responsibility? First of all, your duty is to yourself. How do you serve yourself if you participate in killings and perhaps get yourself killed? Do you serve you or do you serve those who are in political and economic power?

Do you know that there is a higher power, much higher than political or economic? It is the power of your convictions from your heart. It is the power of your being in your own centre. It is the power of a spiritual being, as that is what you are.

You are a spirit living in a cloak of flesh, bones and skin, on your planet called Earth, learning and remembering your origins. How long do you want to continue as such? How long are you going to deny yourself the recognition of who you are? How long are you going to keep taking one step forward and two steps back? How long are you going to keep on coming back, making the same mistakes, taking the same lengthy side roads? Decide for once and for all that you are in the centre of your power coming from your heart and act like it. Keep on acting like it and it will become your first nature rather than your second nature. It will become so natural, as it is natural to us.

And with that, we urge you to awaken. Awaken and be within, conferring with your heart, showing kindness and understanding to those around you. Urge them to talk to their hearts, to confer with their hearts, to base their decisions on their heart's feedback. We urge you to always strive for it. We urge you to live it.

We urge you to spread this message. Be a messenger of your heart's convictions. Do not worry about ridicule. Stay in your own power, and you will see that your power will become visible, will become respected by those around you. They will know that your convictions are based on the heart.

And with that, we wish you all the best. We wish you your strong convictions. Uphold your beliefs and trust your heart. Believe that this is the way to live. Continue living in such a way that when you meet your maker you need not say, "I lived this way as I needed to cover from being spit on, from being maligned, because I was afraid". Do not be afraid. If you live in fear, you will not be able to set yourself straight. You will not be able to get up to your full height. You will not be able to look yourself in the eye. You will always find excuses, and you will believe your excuses. You will become commonplace and comfortable, as you know that there is always an excuse.

Do not live this type of life. Set yourself straight. Be one to come from the heart, and you will never hurt yourself or others. Your heart is calling you, and has been calling you for some time. Listen to this call. Listen to it and act on it. Do not leave your heart waiting and waiting. Be one with your heart.

Namaste and sayonara. We believe you have had enough Helena. Go and rest. We will talk again.

Chapter Three

Many Faces of the Human Race

In the afternoon, I went back to my computer hoping for the messages to continue. As I sat down and positioned my fingers above the keyboard, the transmission started:

We would like to reminisce about humanity's journey, as this is so important. Many people learn from examples that they can relate to much easier than using any textbook or a discourse on the subject. Bless you child for allowing us to use you as an example to illustrate what we mean by "humanity's journey".

Helena has been on her journey for millennia. This statement is as truthful as it is powerful, if you realize what it means. Everyone's mission, each of your consciousnesses is a thread that is with you throughout all your many lives. Your consciousness is rising, or perhaps not, while you manifest in the physical form on your beautiful planet Earth. Helena was a privileged one many times. She also was a pauper, she was tall and short. Through the millennia, she has done it all. She was a man, woman, mother, father, child; she took on many different roles. Through the millennia, she lived in many forms of consciousness and bodily forms. Through the millennia, she evolved and came back. Further evolutions transpired and she came back again.

Her journey is not that unique. You have all been on the same journey for a long time. Some of you may say, "But I do not desire to come here to inhabit a physical form anymore, I want to be done with it". Well, you will. But guess what? There always will be another step, so be patient. Patience is needed, and with patience and letting go of trying to speed up your spiritual progress, a lot can be accomplished.

Every bit of your experience adds a flavour of its own and inches you forward, toward the realization of your spiritual self. Together, all experiences mesh in the way of a growing realization that oh, yes, the 3-D is beautiful but... is there more? Is there that something called the afterlife? To some of you it may seem that these are straightforward questions, but do not be fooled. If these questions are answered and understood, consciousness takes a qualitative leap. This qualitative leap is so powerful that it becomes the milestone of looking at lives, events and interactions with a different understanding.

Helena, today, at this point in her game (oh yes, it is a game you play with yourself), knows that life is continuous and that life never ceases. But then what is the next step? The next step is to ask oneself: "With this knowledge I possess now, how and what I can do to improve this lot of mine? How do I bring the understanding from within, without?" And then something called a path, a life purpose, a life rhythm, starts kicking in. The school of life becomes more and more a testing ground.

You cannot be tested fully unless you are awakened. At least not to the extent that you can be, once awakened to the fact that you are a spirit living in your body-cocoon on your planet. What the test provides at this point is seeing how well you practice what you understand. How well you live it. How well you use what you know. And if you do not get it, the tests become harder and more severe until you do.

And that is what Helena underwent through her recent illness. A big test of understanding her own power of creation. Of her own thoughts, forming her own life story and creating her own circumstances that were seemingly bestowed upon her by others.

That is what you all need to accomplish—living from the centre of your power. It is essential to your own realization. Doormats, victims, martyrs–these are no ways of achieving liberation from the 3-D scenario. No push-overs, no intimidators either.

Compliant to where you are, your tests come and you pass them eventually. Sometimes many hints come along and that is enough to awaken you. If not, then a bigger and more strenuous circumstance will materialize.

This is a general description of the process of realization that Helena went through. We must say, yes, it was more severe than usual as this being named Helena is not unaware, but is surely set in her ways.

So, with this let us go on:

Musta la ti ake? Seti la? Dir nu meti o me. Sur na me kule, e ti si tu a oh. Malino restup pi. Eti ke mani vi lati si note.

We can attest to the miracle of realizing that higher reason always underlies any event. So it applies to sickness. Helena realized what was ailing her and what this higher reason was. She was able to recover with a higher purpose on her mind. Her relationship with her partner improved immensely, and she released a vast amount of hurt and guilt. The dreary nights of Helena's illness brought her the freedom of expressing all of her pains. That is what the test was about.

Do you realize your own potential? Do you know yourself? Do you know that which is embedded in you and keeps on hurting you? Do you know that you can walk away from all the debris that weighs on you after you realize it? Search within and answer all your questions. Release all that hurts you and send a lot of light and love to replenish the space formed by the release. It is that simple. Or difficult, depending on where and who you are.

Resolutions can be little steps or one big upheaval. Your choice and your temperament, or the available circumstances dictate how you choose to do your release. The healing is permanent if that is what you are after. If you need to retain some of your "stuff", you may experience a subsequent crisis. Your need to be in a clear space drives it all. If for any reason you think you need to hang on to any circumstances that in the end will cause pain, you will.

Such is the final transformation that one does not need ever worry about going through a similarly painful experience. The realization is clear. We wish that similar experiences, or rather similar results, be bestowed upon those who have been close to realizing their own part in the creation of events that turned against them in the end. The cleansing power of realizing that, will free the body and mind from following the same pattern and they will be rejuvenated.

Why are we bringing up this point? Such an event en masse can rejuvenate a large portion of inhabitants of the Earth, and from the ashes of their experiences, a bright future will beckon. Beacons of such experiences will light that which was there before, but was obstructed and hidden. Cataclysms of any kind have far reaching consequences and bring seeds of life that is new and not of old. This perhaps may seem a drastic way of obtaining illumination, but through tests of such harsh degrees, you reach realization. Your capacity of understanding your own creation and role is enhanced and will not be reversed, as this realization is profound.

We do not advocate suffering, but if such is needed, if such an event will propel you onto the path of awakening, so be it. Remember, choices are yours. It is not us or any other power that is directing or controlling you. Choices are yours.

Should you need to advance and awaken, an event of testing and suffering will advance you to where you are meant to be, on your path to a great and more enjoyable way of life.

Rest assured that the power of enlightenment is so profound that you will never slide back to your previous way. Rest assured that your experience will enhance your life skills. Rest assured that you will become a lighthouse for others who may or may not need to come to their realization through painful tests. You will be their teacher and guide. And along with your role as a facilitator, they will enhance their own facilitating and guiding skills to go on and help awaken others. This will create a chain reaction. More teachers, guides, facilitators will be born, and more of those crossing their paths will be shaken out of their lethargic ways of living.

We are happy to report that this trend is growing and is reaching the mass media. There is a trend for peace and satisfaction in life derived not from owning, but from helping. Not from attaining material goods, but from sharing. The heartfelt feeling of community with those who are in need supports this trend. There is a new era of people coming together and resolving their pains and troubles. This is a way of becoming a society based on compassion.

This type of society is more poised to succeed as a whole. With a compassionate approach to resolving the ills of society, without the greedy approach of owning and not sharing, such a society is equipped to resolve anything by peaceful means, where opposing sides can present their own woes and views. The entire society benefits from the proclaimed resolutions, as any good thing affects the entire collective. Of course, it works both ways. Any bad resolve affects the entire collective. And what it is you want to be affected by? Positive or negative? Rest assured that the choice will become clearer and clearer and you will know which way you want to advance.

And with that our dear, take a break. You can come back to us any time today. We beg you a wonderful day. We love you and cherish you. Amen.

Amen. Thank you for coming.

༺ ༻

*I am back. Thank you for the break. Just as I fin-
ished thinking my thank-you, a message came
from my I Am:*

"Current astrological influences support the reading
and writing of this type of material. Therefore, be ready
to put in some extra effort. Be ready to write more often
and longer." Your I Am.

Now back to our material. Such is the history of people
that they do not live without tragedy and loss of lives.
Without joy transformed to horror. Without love transformed to hate. With the noise of a gun, a bomb, many
die. Many perish. Many suffer. Everyone killed is on everybody's consciousness, as your own consciousness,
combined in a pool with others, allows such atrocities to
happen. Do not befuddle yourself into believing that you
are not responsible. You all are responsible. Your every
little thought of being displeased, being grouchy, being
angry, is added to the entire pool of consciousness and
influences the outcome of the Earth's volatile past and
present. We do not condone any of this. We are merely
describing it as it is.

Your own beliefs may be in disparity with many other
people's beliefs; nevertheless, make your beliefs known.
Uphold your beliefs. Spread your beliefs, as they need to
be spread if they can help. This way you can help spare
lives. Think and send out the seeds of your thoughts. Say:
"These are my beliefs. I believe in a peaceful society.
Calm and peace, joy and peace, are my foremost beliefs.
Love and unconditional love toward my fellow man are
my beliefs. My I Am supports me, and my beliefs are
spread and brought forth, multiplied and enhanced before they join the pool of total consciousness."

Consciously send your thoughts out towards peace and ask your I Am to enhance the power of your thoughts. Make sure that you spread goodwill and love.

Goodwill, love, kindness in all situations. It does not matter if incidents or events are small. Does not matter how small. Each time act from love, from kindness. No quarrels with your family. No hate toward your neighbours. No accusations. No gossip, no, no, no. Only kindness. A kind heart, love and a helping hand. Transform yourself first, then your transformed self will influence others. And bit-by-bit, this will grow and grow. It will connect and sweep the country. It will connect and sweep the planet. It will grow and nurture love and kindness from a seed into a gentle plant, and then into a strong, large tree with strong roots and a long life.

Helena, we need to ask you the following: Are you committed to working with us?

Yes. I am committed.

We need to know further. Are you committed to spending your time working with us, or are you committed to massaging your ego?

I do not intend to massage my ego. I am committed to working with you.

Commitment means that you never forget who you are. You always remember to listen to your inner voice. You always know about your connection with your spirit. You always know your origins are not on your planet. You always keep this in your mind.

Yes, I am committed. It feels good to say this, as it is saying that I am committed to myself. Thank you.

You are welcome. Many thanks for coming today. Be back tonight before 8 pm. Namaste and sayonara. Be well.

৵ ৹

After supper I went back to the computer. As I sat down, I asked for the dictations to continue: I am asking my guides, my angels, my universal friends, the Federation, all those of the brightest purest light to come, to bring messages that are of the highest benefit to all.

Let us discuss a different topic now. The following pages will be about the sanctity of family.

The family unit is very important. From this unit evolves a new being, dependent on the family for nurturing and sustenance. During the growth years, all children express enthusiasm for the world around them. Their enthusiasm quietens by the time they reach their teens, and once adults, their minds are set. How are they formed? By the family atmosphere. By their parents' teachings and their own experiences.

Utmost care needs to be taken when choosing your partners, as once chosen they change your life. Your offspring's lives arc also affected. You may ask, "But don't we choose a partner before we are born?" Yes, you do, and that is the choosing we are talking about.

The family unit is a base unit of society. This unit is the most important building block. Without the family structure, the law cannot be upheld. Through family, the law is developed. The law and the family are tightly interwoven and are a functioning (or not) model for the rest of society. If the law upholds the family, society is upheld.

Why is that?

Because then the family, as a basic unit, thrives.

Family is the very structure from which each individual comes. If the family is strong and well adjusted, then the individual has the same traits. If individuals are strong and well adjusted, then the society is strong. If the society is not upheld by strong individuals, we need to look at the family structure. Is the family coming apart? Is the family upheld? Is the family the most important establishment? Is the family respected? Is the family unit the prevailing basic entity in society?

These are the questions that need to be asked. A strong family supports strong individuals. An honest and respectful family breeds strong and respectful citizens. A society full of respectful, strong and honest individuals is a society that thrives.

Honesty in relationships is important. All is derived from and depends on relationships. Your position in your family, your position at work, these are relationships that you need to honestly and heartily observe and nurture.

City folks may not be as strongly rooted in their families. They tend to move around more. They lose contact with their families. Family contacts are strongly encouraged as they are vital. Do not lose sight of your siblings and parents. Particularly of your parents, as they need to be looked after in their later years. They need your support, not the support of a stranger.

You need to understand that the strength of the family unit sets the strength of the society.

And with this, sayonara and namaste. We love you and we cherish you. Good night.

Good night. Thank you for coming.

૱ ૹ

It was early morning when I started typing again.

During the 2nd World War... dear Helena, why do you think we keep coming back to the 2nd World War? Was it more bestial than others? Perhaps. Was it more traumatic than others? Perhaps. It is because of the way it was conducted; the deceitful manipulation of nations into believing that some races are superior to others was enormous.

This deceit continues. This deceit is what you need to reject. It is what you need to eliminate. Deceit is abuse, which, if not dealt with, will destroy the recovery of the human race. The deceit that some are better than others is ridiculous. That some are performing better than others is ridiculous. That the male brain is smarter than the woman's is ridiculous. That skin colour states one's place in the world is ridiculous. Deceit is just that, deceit. Deceitful is not the way to be. It is a sickness, which if not eradicated, will undermine the psyche of the universal human being.

The notion that the liquidation of a race's heritage can bring the liquidation of a race is not correct. The race survives with or without its heritage. Heritage is a complex web that enlarges the meaning of the race; however, it is not the base for the race's existence. Race existence is built on the recognition of that which is the same and also different from other races.

Many human forms and species originated way back when the Gods of the Universes were designing the best human form. The best human form was being designed to facilitate the forms that were to come later. By working on the best possible form, the door was opened to many forms. Creation was the starting point and then evolution played a role. You want to have the best possible beginnings, don't you? However, there is not just one best human appearance. All are legitimate expressions of God's creative power. All have legitimate reasons for their existence. All are as they are. They are needed to enhance, to enrich the human experience on Earth. Would it not be simplistic and boring if there were only one food, only one animal, only one bird, only one human being? Would not that be too boring and also appalling, as that simplicity would lead to inbreeding on all levels and the eventual loss of the race through unselective breeding? The offspring would not be as healthy as they are now. The solitude of being one homogenous race would be too oppressive. The possibility of many varieties, surprising discoveries of many species (still some to come) may be a key to the survival of you.

Est la ti u? Eti ma li no? At i lo? Deli me na kuli to. Ati me. Ati me. Se ti la seti la. Amonqua rena. Weli to oma. Deli ku si a me. Ame sesi la. Sesi la to ki. Sesi la ti ki. Deli mina u? Sesi la.

Do you understand the meaning of racial tolerance? Not a very good expression. No tolerance is needed. It is acceptance that is needed. Coexistence. Love. Tolerance signifies that you live with something that you do not approve of. That is not the way to live. Tolerance is the lowest possible level of acceptance. What you need to be is not tolerant but lovingly accepting. Lovingly call to each other and say, "You are my brother, you are my sister, and I love you as I love myself." Therefore, be not tolerant, be loving. Without this step in your upbringing, the race, the human race, may not see the blossoming of a new civilization called the Aquarius Age.

Namaste and sayonara. We love you, and we cherish you. Amen.

Thank you. Amen.

Chapter Four

Mother Earth

It was day thirteenth of the dictations, and the transmitting started as soon as I sat at my computer.

Helena, without people like you, we cannot bring through the knowledge. As a receiver, it is important that you keep yourself in good attunement. Your role is vital, and we would like you to be in contact with your higher self at all times. Spend less time reading newspapers and watching TV. Maintain a peaceful and quiet existence on your part.

Less newspaper and TV? Okay, I will manage. Although, I must say I like reading my newspaper while having my breakfast.

You need to find a different form of pleasure. There is no doubt about that.

Understood.

We would like to talk about the interaction of the Earth and human behaviour. Earth, as a living organism, is watching with trepidation the moves and evolution of human thinking. You may say, "With trepidation? Is there fear of human impact?" You can count on it. Mother Earth, as she is your Mother and you are living in her bosom, has been watching you from the beginning of the establishment of your race on Earth. First with love and excitement, and later, still with love but a little more concern.

Mother Earth now knows that beyond everything, the human race has lost its connection, its link with that which is natural, and is pursuing the unnatural. Through splitting and splicing, adding and deleting genes and other genetic material, humans are attempting re-creation with horrendous consequences in sight. The range of experimentation will continue to expand, and ethical considerations and dangers of genetic manipulation will come increasingly to the forefront. As the rate of technical advancement is exceeding that of spiritual advancement, humans could be well on their way to destroying the biological equilibrium of the planet Earth.

Therefore, Mother Earth, all seeing and knowing, is rightly concerned as her citizens are doing themselves into oblivion. They are also undermining her own growth, as her growth and evolution is connected with yours. As all your bodily functions are interconnected and a condition present in one part of your body influences all, so it is between the Earth and humans. All is interconnected, all is one. There is a link that is visible, and there is a link that is invisible. A visible link, for instance being the food supplies, one of the most important for the race. Invisible are the subtle energies that flow and support the structural bodies of all beings living on Earth. Without this energetic support, the physical being is impaired and no amount of food is able to sustain the body.

And that is what you need to be more concerned about, even more than your food supplies. As you discover and realize that the emphasis on food sustenance is overemphasized, you will understand the meaning of this: the energetic flow between the Earth and your bodies is of the utmost importance.

The first consideration must be that you can eat, and that is fine, as we understand your knowledge is steeped in the 3-D. Throughout the book we will work toward the awakening of your understanding of the structures that are not of 3-D but are in 3-D. You may ask, "How that could be? And why are we not taught about this?" Well, you all need understand that some time ago, the ruling class viewed your own empowerment as a threat to them, and you were therefore kept in the dark. Information was withheld and twisted into a comfortable lie to keep the true identity of you and your link beyond this planet away from you.

This section may not be a revelation to many and that is fine. We are seeking to awaken those who are still asleep. We are seeking to awaken those who are wondering and have already been feeling unease and do not understand from where it is coming. This book was also written for those who already know and would like to get confirmation and find out more. If you are among the first ones to read it, be diligent in showing it to others. Buy it for your brothers and sisters. Spread the knowledge. Go on a quest of being a leader and liberator.

Helena, it has gone well so far. Still, you need to abandon you own thoughts a little more. This means do not prejudge, do not sit and wonder what will come next. Just receive and transcribe as best as you can to get the meaning of the information flowing your way. Your contribution as a transcriber is so important to this project that we would like you to be in the background with your mental judging and evaluating faculties stashed away. And with that said, here we go.

It was a night of reckoning. It was a night of terror. It was a night when humanity woke up and had nothing to put on—no warm clothing, no food to eat—as Mother Earth in her fury shed all, all that was piled up on her back, and began to reinstate herself as the queen she once was.

This is the scenario that you want to avoid. There will be calamities, have no doubt about that, but the final chapter will be realized only if you fail to stop your own creations of your mind, where the connection to the Earth has been severed.

And that has been the case many, many times. Greed and economy have overcome kindness and the heart. The well-being of all has been replaced by the well-being of a few. This means that those who are at the other end of the spectrum have plunged into an abyss of being abused, used, misused, exploited, and so on. You must know the picture, don't you? And no, that is not all. All those who have fallen into the uncertainty cycle will constrict their life force and lose their connection with Mother Earth. Such is the concern of Mother Earth of losing the links with her citizens that she will cause a break in this cycle to ensure that history takes another path.

Therefore, the human race is in danger of being overthrown by its own Mother, the Earth. The Earth is pretty close to shedding its coat, being pushed into this by its own inhabitants, the human race. This does not mean total obliteration of the human race, but it can bring a large culling of the human herd.

The Earth is in the last decade of being compliant. The Earth thinks not of returning to where she was, but of new beginnings, once she sheds most of the disorder abruptly and forcefully. This would mean vast areas of unpopulated Earth so that it could regenerate itself. This would mean, of course, many dead and dying in terror and panic. To avoid a situation that would plunge the human race into fear and big losses, we offer this information as one of the tools that can help you arrive at solutions.

The solution is of immense proportions. Humanity is capable of achieving what needs to be achieved, but can we do it within the short time that we have left? A decade is not that much. (Reference to the year 2012, when a shift in consciousness is predicted to take place. At this time human destiny will reach a crossroads: one way will be the continuation of the 3rd dimension, and the other will represent a path to a higher dimension, a 6th Golden Age that the ancients spoke of long ago.) We need many like you to bring the message of not fear, but peace and cooperation.

Vulnerable you are in front of an angry Mother. Vulnerable you are as a race if your numbers are decimated. Vulnerable you are if you cannot understand that your own creation got out of hand, that your own creation is getting back at you. Your own disregard is bringing atmospheric changes, is bringing slides, is bringing hurricanes, is changing weather patterns. Your own disregard is not good for you, for all planetary beings and for planet Earth herself.

Systematic pollution of the waterways. Systematic deforestation. Systematic misdirecting of the streams and rivers. Systematic pollution of food sources. Systematic tampering with the life-giving properties of codes that are embedded in all the living. Systematic under-evaluation of the danger of it all. Systematic over-evaluation of the importance of money. Greed, exploitation.

See the pattern? It must be broken. How? Through raising the collective consciousness. Through explaining the dependencies. Through raising the consciousness of several who in turn will help more. Through us working with those we can reach and who are willing to cooperate with our efforts to turn the tides of destruction away.

Risk is to assume that humanity will understand on its own. A couple of assumptions can be made: number one, humanity is ready to understand the consequences of its own doing; and number two, humanity is ready to turn against those who perpetrate all these crimes of greed against the planet and its inhabitants.

None of this is visible. None of this is ready. Therefore, the raising of consciousness and emotional bodies must happen as soon as possible. It needs to be built up on a large scale, where many receive messages and revelations, and act on them. This does not mean that all will record and write. It only means that there will be a conscious shift in individuals, and that shift will cause another shift to happen, and so on. As momentum gathers, many will have the knowledge and they will all start acting on it at the same time, feeling the strength in numbers.

Enlisting others is of the utmost importance. Spreading the message is imperative to the changing of people's consciousness. Know that this is the number one priority of this century. Turn around the tide of uncaring, of revolting against the natural laws, of not being in the present.

Evaluate your acts. Be ready to attack your own encumbrances through evolution of your spiritual origins. Be ready to enrol your friends and relatives by showing them the work you yourself have accomplished. Be a leader with ideas. Spread them and talk about the importance of the level of consciousness that people are at.

Namaste and sayonara. We will talk again.

Dear Helena, the evaluation of your thoughts is ongoing. We need to be sure that perseverance is there. We need to make sure that we are working with the right person. We need to make sure that the project will be brought into fruition.

I would like to ask a question.

Go ahead, by all means.

Don't you know beforehand whether it will come to fruition or not? Don't you already know if you are working with the right person or not?

Of course we do, however, under any new circumstances, you may choose another direction. You may decide on an alternative course. You have your free will after all. Therefore, constant urging and checking is required. Do you understand?

I do. Still, I think that you already know the end product and the success of it or not.

Yes, of course we know the end product. Of course we know the success of it or not. But we need to make sure that it happens in the right dimension, and at the time and place at which we want it to appear.

Okay, now I understand better.

So let us continue. We need to assess the well being of this planet once more. This planet is a vibrant planet, even with much of its land and water polluted. America is graced by its crown of crowns, the majestic Rockies, where the amazing wonders of the world are hidden. These are unknown to you. They are hidden from the sight and ears of yours. These are the resuscitating systems of the confused world of humanity. These are the bellybuttons of the world. These are the vents to the world of immense beauty. These are the channels to the worlds of renovating, refurbishing, rejuvenation. These, the most majestic of mountains, are connected to the energetic whirls of the dimensions we are working from. These whirls of energy continuously bring new energies toward the world of yours. The beauty of this is that you cannot influence these energy whirls, as they are not operated from where you are but are operated by us. This said, we will not be identifying the source of the energy coming to you.

There are also other such places on your planet; hence the balancing extends across the entire globe. We mention only these as you (the writer) reside in this part of the world. These energy whirls can be shut and opened at will. Our will. They can be diminished or enlarged. They cannot be moved, as they were set according to your Earthly coordinates. Since the beginning of time, these whirlwinds have been operating throughout the entire universe and are visible only to those who coordinate their energy flow within the universe. These keep the planets balanced and functional.

Now, the reason we are writing about this at this point in time is that we need you to be aware of energies that are beyond you. The energies that are balancing, that keep the equilibrium of your planet. Other influences exist but we choose not to address them here.

With the influences such as those described in the previous paragraphs, we can see that the balance of the Earth needs to be restored, as in its present condition the Earth does not have enough strength to benefit from the influences that we send it from time to time. The Earth can benefit most from these if it is balanced in its 3-D environment. We can attest to the diminishing power of our influences through seeing the disrepair in your atmosphere.

This is a main concern of ours, your atmosphere, as it is the bread and butter of your existence. Your breathing is the foremost function of your body, and the cleanliness of the air is very important to your well-being. Without your breathing an adequate supply of oxygen and an appropriate mix of gases, your body will grow weak and even the most nutritious food supply will not fix it.

Since the industrial revolution, pollution has become a priority of ours. Without the energy whirlwinds there would be more damage. However, it is not only we who are responsible for correcting the inadequacies of your air supplies. We need your cooperation in keeping the proper balance. The Kyoto agreement is of great importance and the consequences of keeping it or not are enormous.

The Kyoto Accord is an agreement of the nations of the planet Earth to adhere to certain improvements over a period of time to stabilize the greenhouse effect on the earthly atmosphere and the entire global environment. Implementing practices that reduce and prevent greenhouse gas emissions is imperative. Changes in the Earth's climate influenced by human activities have adverse effects on nature's ecosystems.

The benefits of implementing the Kyoto Protocol will be numerous, from improvement of the environment by restricting air pollutants, to the nations agreeing and working together as one.

So, what really transpired in Kyoto? Most of the nations who participated were visited by their overseeing angels. Their angels worked together with people to bring new resolutions to activate first links into the New Age, the age of humanity's higher consciousness.

You do not believe that stale air is good for you. Why would you then believe that pollutants are good for you? So why don't all accept Kyoto? Because of the greedy business owners? Because of the politicians being paid and bought by business owners? Because of misinformation? Because of carelessness? Because of the attitude of "who cares, I am okay and nothing else matters"? Because of all of the above?

There is so much at stake. Many children of yours may not be able to raise their children safely. The air will become heavy and of the wrong chemical composition. Many will starve for oxygen. Global warming will continue. You will upset the natural balance and will no longer be able to grow the crops you are used to growing. You will not be able to drink pure water and the dryness will bring a shortage of water.

Your livelihood is at stake. So will it matter if some of you will be rich but will breathe corrupted air, will not be able to walk outside in the polluted air, will not have enough water? Malnutrition, thirst, pollution rising everywhere—is this the vision you are looking forward to? Nothing matters more than a sustainable environment, sustainable crops, clean air, clean and plentiful water. The way of life that has been developed over the millennia is at stake.

So what is the problem with Kyoto? Absolutely nothing. Is there a problem with people? Of course—short sightedness, misinformation, fear-mongering; impressionable, uninformed people who buy into misleading propaganda that Kyoto will lower living standards.

Kyoto, as an agreement of people, is an effort in progress by people of the entire Earth. We suggest that that which works for all is more important than that which works for a few. There is nobody who would not benefit from Kyoto. All are to benefit. Let's grow healthy and wealthy in knowing that working together is better than working against each other. Amen and sayonara.

This concludes this section and we would like you to take a rest. Have your breakfast and once you are done, please come back again. Thank you for coming.

Thank you for your dictation.

⋙ ⋘

Helena, diligence is not your virtue. However, an asset is your goodwill. We are pleased to be talking to you today. We are pleased to be your teachers and the requestors of your time. We can come and be with you any time. However, it is beneficial to be working at the same hour each day. Therefore, we would like you to cooperate in keeping with the time. We would like to have your cooperation by your engaging in meditation. That will keep you more open to the forces of the pure light of the spiritual realm.

Let us continue with our dictations.

Intermittent shock waves are coming to raid this world of yours of its stability.

Intermittent shock waves will be responsible for the reversal of your magnetic field, and, at the moment of reversal, the biggest and most alarming events will transpire. These shock waves are not an original idea of yours. They are an original idea of your Mother Earth. She is dislodging most of the material that is clinging to her that is not of the purest form. Its chemical composition has been compromised or tampered with. This matter needs to be purged before the vibrational force finishes the purification.

Alter the vibrations and the impure matter will fall off sideways, you may say. Not so. Altering the vibrations will not materialize any changes. However, it will provide the strength for the agents of change to come and finish what has been started, to help Mother Earth prepare for her journey to the 5th dimension. This matter, by the way, will not be usable any more.

This matter will be "dead", without any consciousness, and will dissipate into a void. This void will contain anything without a consciousness or awareness. That is the true meaning of a void.

This experience in life changes will be drastic one. There will be big losses of human and animal life. There will be big losses of plants and trees as well. But above all, it will offer new beginnings and show that the ways employed by humanity are not sustainable. It will be the start of a new age where the cooperation of races and species will prevail. This cooperation will bring a new golden age where unconditional love will dominate.

Exceptionally high migration of those who decide to leave this planet will soon occur, as large numbers of people have already decided to leave. Why? The reason is multifaceted. They do not want to experience the tribulations that are coming your way. They know that they will not be easy to take and they are not willing to subject themselves to suffering.

Those who will stay will do so because they know that this test is important for them. Others believe that by staying they will resolve their dilemma of not participating in the most exciting event of this millennium – the coming of the era of Aquarius. And those who can bear staying are also doing it out of love for humanity, as many of them are teachers and leaders whose roles are to teach and lead in the time of crisis.

As we have already mentioned, many will leave and many will stay for personal and other reasons. We will not go into this scenario any further, as it is shrouded in mystery even for us. We can only say that this big up-heaval will take many lives and will save many of those who will act at the right time and in the right place. Therefore, the goodwill of those who will stay will save many.

Silu mi na tu? Et la? Duiti kuli me? Anila? Certi tu, certi tu, mia dora. Eti mu eti mu paridiora. Certi tu mia dora, certi tu.

The understanding of those who will leave will be at stake, as their leaving may mean wasting their opportunities for growth and enlightenment. By suffering through this upheaval, many will begin to understand, many will come to understand.

A word of caution: if you think that you need to go, go. That is what your higher self is directing you to do. Do not agonize over your urges and intuition. Just listen to it. If it says go, go. If it says stay, stay.

And with that, we have finished for today. We wish you a nice day and do come back tomorrow. Namaste and sayonara. Amen, and have a good night.

Deli moni seti la. Oki tuli moni ni. Situ oki seli la. Seti la seti la.

Dear Helena, this morning we would like to continue to give a realistic picture of Mother Earth's effort to cleanse and elevate herself into a higher dimension. She is on the way to join the planets that already are in the 5th dimension. She is on the way, concentrating on shedding the images of wars and conflicts from her aura. She has started shedding the images and vile warmongering, and she will shed more and more in the months and years to come. Your Mother Earth is not going to stop until all is back into balance and her role is established in bringing peace to humanity.

Mother Earth's shedding of discord and of undesirable qualities will bring the population of Earth to the realization of the impact of their own contribution to all that they have experienced in the past and will in the future. These experiences are invaluable, as they will create indelible impressions that will be etched in the minds of those who will survive.

There will be an attrition of all who did not get the concept of them being a creator with the supreme God, the creator of all. You create that which you live. You create that which is then bestowed (in your mind) upon you. You create that which is you. You cry in despair and look for solutions, and meanwhile, all solutions are within. Within your heart, within yourselves. Look into the depths of yourself honestly with all your might, bringing that which you find to examine to either cherish or discard. Discard you must. Discard all that is old and does not serve you. Discard all that is obsolete.

Sela tu ami. Nu li mi tu. Esto la kuli minu tu? Esti la, esti la, esti la. Dei sa minu lo te ko mi no.

Atilo peratu sotilo. Elatu mulimu eti ku. Delti o pureme suti tu. Delta mu omi na deli pu oli. Seti mori ako teli. Do ra mu ne ko apoli ko ti moro selo dale api. Nook moi no. Seti pe la. Kuli no? Delti ola molino. Delti pere sula minu ki. Sil ami no tile dori ka teki. Sme na mi nu ate ko vame.

Delta re tu mi no ra ku ti. Polo mi dela mi no ku as ti pelaki. Delta puli omi no. Ka ke? Omina lo ti opu ku si mi nakoti. Esti ma no ke. Esti mano ke.

Resi ku li? Amoni polu na. Meni peru si ako la. Deli mu? Noli ame. Seti ela baluki ome. Seti la. Seti la seti la.

No mi a. Nomi a emeni tu akole to vi re ti mu. Selti o, selti o. Mene mi nau. Se ti opiku. Seti mi, setimi.

Ene ta likula. Seti mene ami no. Setu alo nami re ka. Apoku latomi neti muka rekate dei muli omano ti le. Se ta. Set la, amo.

Desa mena tuli pa. Dista mene alita. Duri mi nula qi o. Seti paremu naqi o. Delta, delta mi. Nuli. Smi no. Seti ku li ote opo. Delti mena mani cotisu emena kuli baste sa pelu.

Reti mu nale to. Rei mu nale me. Seti o seti la, vi a mela novi ku ti o. Ceti la ome no pita si kola ase ro. Meste one o.

Amen. Thank you for coming.

The chemicals developed during the 2nd World War were to be used on the enemy. Now they are for the entire world. They were for the enemy and now you are the "enemy"—you are the consumer, you are the user. You can and are getting poisoned.

The chemicals are now used without much restraint in household cleaning supplies. They are used in pesticides and fertilizers. The consciousness of people making these is not at all with the population. The consciousness of these people is of a low grade and will not be of an enlightened state until they see their wrongdoings.

During the 2nd World War, the mind was set to punish the enemy. Many people were killed and the newspapers wrote about it in superlative ways such as: "The Enemy Is Destroyed". In the ensuing years, the mind was set to use the chemical supplies and make more to sell for profit. The fanfares died and became silent. Now you kill your own and there is nothing to brag about. The silent chemical killers bring the money in. Corporate profits soar. Profit is all. Money wins. Money clears everything. Everything and anything is justified by profit, even a silent murder.

Such is the transgression against the peoples' rights to live, that Mother Earth is not sure how much cleansing will be needed to activate the healing power of nature. Toxic sediments can be withdrawn from the earth and refurbished into non-toxic material by the power of transmuting the energetic and vibrational levels of these compounds. Through the power of transmutation, the resulting matter is without a doubt clean of toxins. Mother Earth has all the power to transmute that which is toxic and a storehouse of sicknesses and maladies, for centuries to come. However, the transmutations need to match the consciousness of the citizens of Earth.

And why is that?

Because, through transmutations, the toxins are no longer but the machinery that brings them back still exists. This is not a cycle you can stay in. The way out is not through transmutation. The way out is through raising consciousness, through raising awareness. When such a process takes root, the results are supported by Mother Nature, and she can contribute through transmuting existing chemicals stored in her water and soil.

Helena, please try to quiet your mind. Do not interfere. Try to overcome your chattering mind. Stare at the keyboard and type mechanically without paying attention to the words. As the words come, type without connecting them into sentences in your mind.

I'll give it my best.

Good. Your mind is operating but it is quieter. This is better. We are continuing.

Dala mitu ke. Tira milo me. Oti ku ta li? Oti se mi? Deka nu alo petiko si.

Those living on Earth at this time have one underlying lesson: awareness. Awareness, through raising the entire population on Earth toward a new level of awareness, toward the self-conscious realization of principles based on love, not on exploitation and greed. This era of upheavals will drive this home and many people will be shaken from their lethargy, from their cocoon of self-satisfaction. The wave of awakening will wash over the entire globe and will stir more and more people. Such times are rare and will not come often. Thus, the entire population needs to play out its role and be shaken into the realization that the ways implemented and used at present cannot continue, as the lives of people cannot be sustained by such practices.

Helena, how are you doing?

I am doing well, thank you.

Tired?

No, I feel fine.

Good. We wish that you take a break and have your breakfast. Be back before 10 am.

Thank you. See you soon.

The layers and layers of abuse against the environment and living organisms are alarming and cannot be discarded without help. We, as the planetary logos of this universe, are ready to be of assistance if humanity allows us to help with the changes. These changes are crucial. Raising your consciousness to a needed level will support the changes. Otherwise, the level of your consciousness will lag behind the changes and that is not what we are after.

We, of course, can only achieve this if you are willing to cooperate. There is nothing we can do as your will is foremost to any other kind of intervention.

The changes cannot be brought on before the raising of your consciousness. And your consciousness cannot be raised before you understand the difficult situation you are in.

Understand that you need to change to save the human race and the planet. It is that simple—you are sliding further than you can comprehend right now. Do not be ready to obliterate yourself. Be ready to conquer yourself. Be ready to go on to your intended greatness. Be ready to go on to your intended salvation through your ascension, passing through an inter-dimensional portal to the 5th dimension. This is the theme of this century—ascension.

Preparation has been underway and the seriousness of the situation is calling for reinforcement of those who understand the gravity of the situation. Be ready and willing to change. Be ready and willing to help those who do not understand. Be ready and willing to elevate yourself by raising the level of your consciousness.

What does this mean? It means working from your heart charka. Simply said, from your heart. Your heart knows. Your heart is ready to step forward. Your heart is the leader and is willing to pick up its leadership role. Do not assess anything without bringing your heart into it first. If it does not feel right, if it will inconvenience somebody, if it will hurt someone, if you are not sure that your intent is noble and honourable, do not proceed. Your heart knows. Listen to your heart. Listen to your mind not. Your heart is the way to connect with your higher self, with that part of you that you forgot about while on Earth. Your higher self is watching and waiting for the opportunity to connect with you, and what better way of doing so than being and acting from your heart. You heart is the one that you need to listen to.

We are here and are fading away, as there are others we need to go and talk to. Our mission is a mission of bringing the truth and change to humanity before it is too late. And with that we can say that the transmitter, Helena, is doing a great job and we are pleased to be working with her.

Helena, see you again early tomorrow, at 8 o'clock in the morning.

Yes. Thank you for coming.

And that is all for today. We love you and we cherish you. Amen.

Chapter Five

Your Heart Is Calling You

This chapter will be a change from the direction we were taking before. This chapter may be ground zero for many people—it all depends where the person is.

But before you continue we would like to assess how you feel Helena. Is anything ailing you?

> *My legs are hurting today. They are painful all the way down to my ankles.*

Right, let us relieve the pain. Sit and relax for a few moments and let the light be present in your legs. Imagine the presence of the light flowing through your body and washing out the pain from your legs.

> *Yes. I feel relief, thank you.*

You are welcome. So, without further ado, let us start our dictations.

Your heart as an organ has its counterpart. It is an ethereal heart, which is in charge of the physical heart. This ethereal heart of yours is connected to your planetary heart. All the way to Spirit and God your heart is linked. It pumps your blood. It makes you love. It is your best advisor. It is your leader.

Your heart is all you need to overcome your difficulties. Bring your heart into all your actions and you will see amazing changes. Do not ask, "Can I do it? Will this and that person like what I do?" Ask your heart: "How do you like it heart? Does it feel good? Is this the right thing to do?"

You will be surprised at the accuracy of your judgment. You will never snub or spoil anyone. You will never decide on something that will come back to haunt you. You will never have to regret your actions or resolve an awkward situation.

Be within and examine your motives. Your motives are creations of your mind that will show you if your heart is leading you or not. Are your motives noble? Or do they cover deeper motives, which are the real motives for your taking a certain action? Is there a motive that is showing you your true potential for working with your heart, or is there a motive that is showing you that you need to uncover a layer of motives to find your heart? Is it still alive and warm? Is it cold and hurting? These are the questions you need to work with.

Your heart needs to be uncovered. Your heart needs to be visible. Your heart needs to be found. Go and find it. This is the most important act of your life. When you find your heart support it, nurture it. Be kind to your heart. Your heart will show you its strength. Your heart will support you and lead you. Your heart will show you the way. Be kind to your heart and your heart will reward you.

Use your heart; that is the way. Put your heart first and you will never be lost. Statements that are purely from the mind are shallow interpretations of reality that is qualified by your opinions. Shallow interpretation does not work; immersing yourself is a better approach. If you do not mean what you say from your heart, it is meaningless.

Do not regret what you say. Examine it for what it meant when you said it. Learn from it. By being in your heart, you cannot and will not repeat anything you have already done that did not go well or that hurt people. If you only examine it intellectually, it will not sink in as much as it would if you were to examine it with your heart. Your heart will not allow you to commit the same offence again.

Working from your heart is the most important lesson of your life. If you get this, you will get all. If you do not, you will come back and try again.

Sometimes it takes many tries but all will make it. The timing is not something you need to worry about. The timing is custom-made for you. Why do you think you were not ready? Because you were not ready. It is that simple.

The following may feel like a digression: while your time is tick-tocking, our time is not. Qualitative steps measure our time from one epoch to another. Your time moves on and on, with or without the qualitative changes. It is measured automatically, mechanically. You will change from one century to another, and you will move on time-wise. Whether you progress or not, you will move on. Heartfelt actions do not manage your time driven world. You do not use the heart as a measure of your moving from one epoch to the next. With heartfelt action, you will see that your progress is there. Without the heart, you may feel that you progress as well, but because of the way you measure time, you are unable to see the difference. Sometimes you delude yourself into believing that progress is happening, but all is simply moving on as you measure your time.

Your time measures where you are, not the quality of your actions. Being on time is something that is important to you. Being on time is a measure of respect for others. Being on time is important in a business relationship. It is a hindrance if you are late. Your tick-tock time is important to you. Such is your way of living that without time you feel lost. You wear your watches. You wear them on your wrist, around your neck. Your watch drives your day. You eat on time, you get up on time, you go to work on time.

What are we driving at? With a heart driven society, time will be more of a checkpoint of your day instead of that "very important" quality which you need to assess – being on time. With heartfelt actions, progress is faster as you avoid all pitfalls and events that you need to remedy. You will find yourself with more time on your hands. You will be less tied up by meetings, communications, explanations, and so on.

Put your heart to work. It is waiting to be used. It is pining for you. It is yours to become your best friend and ally. Take time to discover your heart and your heart will reward you with giving you some of that time back. Be a winner. Let your heart lead you.

This is the end of this dictation. We believe you have had enough. Go and rest. We will talk again. Namaste and sayonara. Amen.

❧ ❧

Seti la seti la. Bis aka masit ur.

During the 2nd World War, we were not sure if the Earth would survive, as the spirit of humanity was bogged down with hatred. The human race was engaged in conflicts and the bubble of hatred had swallowed many. It was a time of survival and conquering.

The bubble burst, only to start growing again. Hatred is once more prevalent. Misguided national pride, misguided pride in the war machines that control the world are widespread.

Ceci no bi. Tu i so?

During the 2nd World War, the heart chakra closed. Permanently was the plan.

The plan?

Yes, of those who are a leading force of the dark.

What do you mean by a leading force of the dark?

The forces of dark operate from their lower abdominal region, from the lower chakras. They do not subscribe to the universal law of unconditional love. Their intent is to destroy all that is of light. They are intent on spreading hatred and are not interested in raising the energies and the light of humanity. Their aim is to defy the light and extend the entire world into darkness.

Seti la ome no pera tu ti sece la sila. Seti la oke no mi sela pe ti tu reo.

Your outbursts of hatred challenge your progress. Hatred is all that is not pure love; that is what it is.

The heart is a leading subject of ours, as the heart is something humanity needs to work on. Your heart chakra is the most important aspect of you. Your heart is the most important one in your evolution now. It is the centre of unconditional love, forgiveness and compassion for all inhabitants of Earth. It is a lighthouse that can lead you to riches of mind and body, to riches of money. It is the connection between physical and spiritual.

This transmission is not about the human chakra system as such. We would only like to discuss the alignment and the relationship between the 2nd and heart chakras, as now it is time to balance both of these chakras. Without this balance, the spirit cannot come to full fruition. *Ceci la. Meti oke no?*

The 2nd, sacral chakra has no origin in your sex organs. It is not at all simply your sexual centre. It supports the sexual organs, the centre of physical creativity, the master gonad centre for procreation of the physical kind. The 2nd chakra is a powerhouse from where the main energy flows.

What do you mean by the main energy?

We mean the energy that drives your physical being. It is sent to you through Mother Earth. Through the universal cycle, it comes to your planet. It is refurbished by the Earth and then passed onto you.

Your creative power comes from the 2nd chakra. Your creative juices flow from this centre and are dependent on the state of the 2nd chakra. The 2nd chakra is a spiritual centre to your creative self; and without it, your creative side is not. Your entire creative ability is connected to this chakra. It is a centre of expression for sexuality and creativity, and the physical and mental creative sides of you come from this centre.

Regarding the 2nd and heart chakras, your world is mostly driven either by one or the other. You need to balance them together. One needs to support the other. Realize that a sexual relationship without input of your heart is meaningless.

You do not want to live a meaningless existence. Not even one meaningless occasion. Vibrationally speaking, your heart chakra should lead all your activities. Therefore, the support of your other chakras for your heart chakra is needed. Without reviving the sacral, or 2nd chakra, you will not help your heart chakra.

How do you balance the 2nd and heart chakras? Think of your sexual chakra as creative, loving, releasing and giving. Think of your heart chakra as loving, releasing, giving. Is there a difference? Not really, they are similar.

How do you revive the 2nd chakra? Through love for your partner. Through unconditional love. Giving yourself to him or her, through unconditional love. The 2nd chakra opening to welcome your partner is a joyful occasion as the creative side of you is expressed. No partnership can work if the taking or giving is one sided. However you look at it, your life is about partnership. Therefore, in having a partner, you have a responsibility to bring the element of caring from both partners into the relationship.

> How do you revive the 2nd chakra if one does not
> have a partner?

There are different partnerships. The sexual relationship is one of them. Stability of partnership comes through balancing. All partnerships need to be balanced.

You need to understand that the creative side, physical or not, is the expression of the 2nd chakra. The 2nd chakra is not only about sexual relationships. When you express the creativity by giving your creative input you will be exposed to the other side, to whoever will be recipient of you creativity.

> I am not sure if I am clear on this. When you said: "... Through love for your partner, through unconditional love. Giving yourself to him or her...", it sounded like you were talking about a sexual relationship.

The revival of the 2nd chakra comes through opening the 2nd chakra to your partner regardless of the type of partnership. You extend unconditional love to your partner in your life, being it your sexual or any other relationship.

For instance, suppose that you are a creative type. You would like to share your creativity with others. You invite people, such as publishers, to bring your creations to the public. In this case, the partnership needs to be friendly and trusting, not suspecting or distrusting. Another example is that you need to trust and respect the gallery owner if you want to exhibit your paintings. You want to work closely with your publisher or gallery owner if you want to publish your article or book, or exhibit your paintings.

You want to give and receive. This is the same for all relationships. To love, give and receive in a sexual relationship or any other relationship. That is all. *Cela si me no api? Certi meno k? Desti mae nope.*

Shy yourself from an exploitative relationship. Approach all with unconditional love and trust. Open your creative centre, your 2nd chakra. Be in touch with your feelings. Do not expect to receive without giving. *Ceti u? Desti mone aki ma. Delti oke mi.*

It is the nature of some humans that they control the 2nd chakra from their beastly side.

Beastly side?

Yes. Beastly, like in animal. Since you lost sight of your divinity, the 2nd chakra, the sacral or sexual chakra, has been misaligned or misused by many. It has been confused with the power centre, as many came from the 2nd chakra to threaten their partner or the opposite sex. It is still being used as a tool of power over others.

The animalistic perception of the 2nd chakra surrounds the entire misconception of the power of sex.

How preposterous of you to think that that is what keeps you young. Your heart keeps you young. Your heart is the one that propels you, not sex. Sex, when used without the heart chakra, drains vital energy that needs to be replenished. When used with the heart chakra energy, it is the most uplifting experience. When the 2nd chakra connects with the heart, it is a joyous experience. The heart chakra connection with the 2nd chakra is very important, without which sex is meaningless.

We could not be more certain that now is the time for balancing the 2nd and heart chakras. Your heart is the leader of your life and needs to be prominent.

Like being in love?

The heart chakra is beyond being in love with someone. It is being in love with yourself, with the whole of creation. It is being thoughtful and kind. It is being assisting and helpful. It is being right there when someone needs uplifting. It is being ready to lend a hand to yourself and to others.

And that is all for now. We love you and we cherish you. Amen, and see you later today.

୬୨ ୨୬

Veti ali mano ke, se tu rami name si? Del ti umantikoa. Suti aremino pa. Delti, delti, delti.

Credentials are always good but sometimes not enough. Credentials are a curious way of proving your credibility to undertake an action, to undertake an employment position. Credentials assure (or not) that the person is eligible to present herself in the way of saying: "I am credible, I am educated and experienced to take this position on, to take that post. I am the right person."

Credentials of education and experience do not guarantee that a person is capable of being in a leading authority role. This is so when the person does not come from his heart. If the person does not come from a heart position, his views and actions are mind driven. The actions may then repel success, even though they appear to be the right way of achieving the desired result. It may take a long time to recognize that such an individual is not capable of delivering the wanted results. Why are they not capable? The heart is not there. The heart is missing. The heart is not activated.

The heart is so important that without heart driven activity and ideas, the result is not what it could be. Aladdin's lamp is a prime example, used as a miracle worker that failed to deliver happiness. Why? Because a tool as powerful as that is misused once the heart is not present and greed kicks in. Such is the power of the heart, such is its role.

By not living from the heart, humanity has been declining ever since their starting the industrial revolution. The aspects of the heart were forgotten. The aspects of the heart were suppressed. During the 2nd World War, many of you came from fear. Fear was widespread and the heart was not used. It is time to use the heart, to put your heart into all your doings. Your heart is a very powerful organ that was designed multi-purposely. Go and activate all of its functions.

We are calling on all of you to come and listen to this call for the freeing of the heart. We are calling on you to examine your motives. Is your heart leading you or not? By clearing the background motives, your heart, if suppressed, will recover and you will see the world through your heart's way. Your heart is naturally good. Your heart has no other way of living. Through the goodness of your heart, you will recognize evil from good. Evil will have no chance against the heart. Such is its power.

Examine recent events in your life and find out how much your heart participated. Was it engaged or not? Was it at the forefront or not? Answer honestly and you will unravel the way onto the path of self-liberation from the influences of greed or lack of any kind — money, relationships...

That which is off balance, lack or excess, is the result of your heart being suppressed, your heart not being the leading factor of your life.

Se la mi talu? Ali ku pina ti? Sesi su.

Your heart is calling you through the fragments of your lives. The heart is calling, is asking to be recognized. All the pining for something better, for finding yourself, as you like to call it, is the call of the heart. It is calling you to rediscover yourself, to find that little push, more and more, further and further, until you know that the heart is your friend, your ally.

This needs to be done in one sweeping motion, throughout entire countries. This needs to be done by as many individuals as possible. Thus, it is important to spread this message to many. Show these passages to all that are around you. Talk about the heart being a multifaceted organ that not only delivers blood, but delivers a better, more balanced life that will soothe you, that will lead you toward your full realization as a human being who is aware, who is never alone, who is happy and joyful, who is not aloof, is not uncaring.

May you be winners by finding your hearts. May you be people who start this revolution. Find your heart. Find your heart and see the difference. Find your heart.

Namaste, and take a break. We love you and we cherish you. Amen.

Desti ma ni ou ti la. Ani mati durila. Keti la? Keti la? Duri minu ope rate buli senu ai nate. Deli ma deli ma. Deli ku ma na. Ati pole se na. Mati la. Ma it la.

During the 2nd World War, there were prisoners of war that were treated casually, and there were those who were treated brutally. Man's nature has not changed. It is known that practices are still brutal whenever prisoners of war are captured.

We need to say the following: this is a book of grievances not; rather, it is about self-modification. About self-learning to become your best, about self-determination to raise awareness and become conscious of the atrocities the human mind is capable of. With this awareness, the thoughts and implements that support such behaviour may be eradicated.

With kindness to yourself, spread the kindness to your immediate surroundings. Then, taking it further, you can and will change how you are now, and become what you are—a being of pure light, coming from God.

This statement needs to be remembered: do not believe that you are a beast. Nothing can be as "beastly" as a human being, yet that does not make you a beast. You are a being of pure light that is caked in many layers of reincarnations. You are a pure blessed soul that is waiting for salvation, which does not come through someone or something, but through your own self.

Therefore, be ready to work on that which is your first (spiritual) nature, and may you be aware of your faults, and may you uphold yourself to the level of purity you were meant to be.

Sesi mo? Dali tu li oki nu. Me ti na le osi tu. Delti oh, delti oh. Your I Am is conversing with you. Do you feel the sweetness and warmth of those syllables? Do you understand that the force to be kind is immense everywhere? In all universes, all dimensions, places and timelines. You are in the centre of all this kindness that is bestowed upon you. Do you understand that? Be like a feather when dealing with yourself and people around you. Be strong, firm, but featherlike. Just like a feather, light and strong to function. Be featherlike, smooth and soft. Can you be like that? Can you do it?

Of course you can, as that is your real nature. How does it feel to be kind? The warm feeling? Oh yes, it is such a warm feeling. All need kindness and love. All yearn for it. All crave it. All need that feeling of belonging. Feeling embalmed in a cocoon of love is the best feeling you can give to yourself. Be strong as a feather. Be smooth and soft as a feather. Be kind to yourself and those around you.

You can change intense anger, subsiding it to a small feeling of discomfort. See for yourself by calming your anger about something that is unavailable to you. Send love from your heart toward the perpetrator of the event that you felt was sprung upon you. Then feel love growing and pulling you toward the person or object of your displeasure. Once the love reaches them, the event dissipates. Allow yourself to feel relief, and anger will never be your companion.

Use a similar approach with other negative notions. Be aware of your feelings. Examine them for what they are.

Your feelings, if accosted before known to those around you, can be changed or modified. This will enhance the traveling of your love to other members of society. This will not be conceited. This will be a heartfelt exercise in checking your negative feelings and emotions.

We would like to point out that this so-called anger is an inability of yours to deal with a presented situation that cannot be dissipated by that anger. Your anger is no more than a little bandage for your aching and hurt ego. So be smart and allow yourself to observe and examine what you feel. Once you understand you can let go, then, by applying this approach, you will never be drawn into arguments and fights, verbal or physical. This is the power of love. This is the power of a serene, wise person.

You can be like that any time. You can be like that, as you already have a seed of all in you and can acknowledge your negative emotions and allow them to dissipate before they erupt. You can change them. If not, then get them all out, as release is important. Once they are out, do examine them to realize why and what happened there. In the end, you become the boss of your own emotions and feelings.

And why not? They are yours. So be their boss. That is what your role is. The boss of your body, of your emotions. You are the king of yourself. Do not let emotions and your body run you. Hear us? Do not let them run you, you run them. Be in charge of that which is yours.

Amen and see you tomorrow. We love you and we cherish you. Namaste.

You keep a stiff upper lip. You keep your cool. You keep your awe of others. You keep your reserved nature. You keep, keep, keep. Do you see what we mean? You spend energy on keeping, keeping, instead of flowing. Flow. Be in flow. Do not be impeded by a feeling that you always need to look right. That your dress is not short or long enough. That your socks do not match. Be in flow.

What a relief. Relax and experience joy. The joy of being in flow. With yourself, with your surroundings, with your loved ones. Being in flow is the way to be.

Delve into the harmonies, delve into the feelings, delve into all that is connected to the heart.

Delve into that which is not mental. Which is supreme to mental; which is a connection via the heart to your supreme being, creator of creators, God. By delving into the values linked to the heart, you can and will be in more direct connection with His energy. You will be more in tune with your own energy. You will hear others through your heart, not your mind. You will feel instead of judge. You will know without reasoning. You will be in the flow of energetic fields and will choose all that sustains you, that calls you, that is you, as that is what we all are. We are a flow. We are a flow of consciousness, of energy. We are a flow, and being in flow, we are like fish in water.

Flow is where we are, where we live. When we enjoy ourselves by being in flow we become that flow and seep from one to another. We feel the unity, we are one. Where there is flow there is no separation. Fluidity has no beginning and no end. Therefore, you can be a tree's conscious brother. You can walk during your day looking at things through a deer's eyes. You will see your partner as the unity you are. This is the joy of living. This is the joy of not being separated from each other. This is the joy.

How do you know if you are in flow? To see if you are in flow, examine the way you feel. Are you anxious or not? Are you expectant or not? Are you hyper or calm? What is your feeling around places, people and so on? Are you impatient with them, are you rushing events, are you not listening to people, are you not seeing their anguish or joy?

These are all indications of your flow. Flow and there is no anguish, rushing, or impatience. All is calm and taken in a state of pleasantness, calmness and peace.

Being in flow is the way to be. Being in flow is soothing to your nerves, calming to your body, calming to the people around you. Being in flow is so mellow that, to you, all problems feel like they have no weight. They are not weighty. They are not important. Your life flows like a brook in a meadow through the right circumstances.

If you are in flow, it will affect all people around you. They will be in flow by you getting in flow. All will be in flow around wherever you move. You will be in flow on all levels of your existence. You will be at peace. Your body will be at the highest peak possible of its restful self. You will never be rattled and events will slide in and out of your life, as they should, without too much event-fullness.

That is how to live your life. Flow, flow, flow. Flow with the energy within, with the energy without. Flow, flow, flow. Energies flow with those surrounding them. Synchronicity is the result of flowing your energies in harmony with the energies around you. That is how synchronicity happens. Then synchronized harmonic energies begin synchronized harmonic events in your life, and more synchronicity takes place.

Realizing that flow brings you revelations is pertinent to your life. Flow is where intuition and knowledge come from. You will know where you need to be, what to do, how to act, how to react. Your flow will bring to you that which you worked on so hard with so much effort, effortlessly. "Be in flow" is a message that needs to be spread. Being in flow is letting your divinity take over to work the circumstances out, seemingly by themselves. Being in flow is the flow itself.

Get yourself sliding, flowing with the flow around you, as that is where you need to be, as all that is around you is important to you. Otherwise, it would not be around your space. See the connection. Let the events, places, people unravel around you. Let them experience their flow the way they understand it and experience yours the way you understand it. Is there a clash? So be it. Do not dwell on it. Let it pass from your space and stay in your own space. Do not enter the clash's space.

Do you understand? It is all about you, not about others. It is about you, not them. Stay in your flow, in the centre of your own power. No other person can influence you once you recognize the peace you can live is yours and is not changed by anybody else.

You do not need to lay the law down. You do not need to overpower anybody. You do not need to make any demands. You do not need to order or ask. You are all that you are without anybody having to comply with you. To assist you. You can be all yourself and so can they.

Let yourself unravel in your full capacity, and then mountains become molehills. Raging rivers become little streams. Problems disappear and you will never miss them or want them back.

Be in flow. There is nothing you need or have to do. There is nothing you ought to do. All is as it is. You do what your desire tells you to do, not because of others but because of your own desire to be there, to do what you want to do.

Always ask. Ask your heart. "Why am I asking for it? Why do I want it? Do I need it? Do I need to feel good because some other person will like what I do? Is it for me? Is it because of my own idea, or is it someone else's idea I think I need to look after?" And then you will be clear on what you need to do.

Be in charge, examine your want. Find whose want it is, your own or someone else's. Then act or not, you decide. Stay in flow and life will be a pleasant stroll in the meadows.

And that is all for now. Namaste, and we will see you later. We love you and we cherish you. Be in flow. Are you?

Resonance in the heart is the biggest echo of your yearning for fulfillment. Resonance within your heart is your guidance. Do I like it? Is my heart singing? Is my heart sad? Is my heart confused? Is my heart wilting? Is my heart joyful? Pleased? Playful? Happy?

These are the indicators of resonance. How the event resonates in your heart. How the words you hear resonate in your heart. How the meaning of what you sense resonates in your heart. Is the resonance something that feels good? Is the resonance pleasing? Is the resonance filling you with joy?

When you answer these and similar questions, this will let you know how well you can become a part of the scenario, of the event. If the resonance is not a pleasant one, do not participate.

If you doubt your feeling, examine deeper and decide. What is it I feel and why? How is my love of this? Is it easy or difficult? Is it joyful or not? Go by these indications and you will never be in error. Resonance is quite a sophisticated tool on your part. You need no more. Examine the feelings you have and be ready to partake or not. Ask, and all your questions will be answered. Ask, and you will be given.

Helena, this morning we invited you to ask for something and you asked for this material to be published. Your wish is being granted. Do you like it?

Yes, it feels good and I feel happy.

That is resonance. This is something that pleases you, so partake in it. You will succeed and be driven to produce more, which is what we would like to do as well.

Nemesis is if you want to do too much. Remember, love what you do. Do not overdo or overcompensate for not being in flow. Do not push yourself. Take it as it is given to you. Rest assured that all that needs to be done will be. Be in flow and be happy.

If you feel that you can do more, ask. We will observe and you will know our answer. But best of all, be happy with what is happening right now. Do not ask for more right away. Observe and learn from the process. Be in contact with us. Be willing and flowing in your wanting to work with us. Helena, be in flow. You are at the best place you could be. You are at home talking to us, writing a book. You are making progress in delivering this material to those who want it, and that is what we want to write about.

Be assured that all that needs to be published will be. There are many people who have been waiting for this material. Consciously or not, they are waiting. They want to hear this, they want to use it, they want to know it. The expectations will be high. Do not be disappointed if some of them will not be happy with your offer. Do not be disappointed and remember, it is written for those who will appreciate it. If they do not, it was not written for them. It is that simple.

Do not hesitate about continuing if you see reactions that are not pleasant. Be in tune with the pleasant reactions. A joyful, pleasant resonance is stronger than a haughty, unpleasant one. Therefore, those who cannot read what you write will not. They are not ready to consider this material worthy of their attention and that is where they are. Their attention is clued in to a different angle than this.

Be aware of mixed reactions and be ready to accept those that resonate right for you; otherwise, you will not feel good and this will influence your further output. This is not a warning. This is a friendly reminder of things to come.

And with that, have a good night and be ready to talk to us tomorrow at 8 am. Namaste and good night.

Good night and thank you.

You are welcome.

Chapter Six

Be in the Centre of Your Power
The Creator Is You

Desi mi na ti. Oki ti lo? Sel ti. Amo.

Your I Am is calling you. Your I Am is speaking to you. "Distance yourself from that which is not of primary interest to you. Believe that you can be all that you need to be and you will. Be within, and without will be taken care of." Your I Am has spoken.

Such is the nature of humanity that it does not know. Such is the nature of humanity that it is separated. Such is the nature of humanity that it is seeking, it is looking for answers. It wants to know, to realize the power within.

Es ti la? Desi ku? Me ti oni? Eti ku? Lesi pu ta mi?

And the questions are numerous. The questions are many. The questions are difficult and then they are not. The difficulty is in the person herself. The difficulty is in the beholder.

As tu mu? Se ti e? Et tu la? Et ti anu? Et ti la? Et ti anuma? Et ti o mu ku pa?

The universe replies. It follows. It obeys. It nullifies your fears if you nullify them yourself. It approves of you if you approve of yourself. It echoes you. It asks not. It always replies.

You need to ask. You need to search. You need to ask and search. You will be given the answer.

Trust the process. Trust and listen to you. Listen to your intuition. Do not expect a big voice to come down from the sky to bring you the answer. Listen to your quiet little voice within. Approach it with a child's abandon. With a child's trust. Trust the process. Trust the universe. And above all, trust yourself.

Put yourself on a pedestal of self-love. Love yourself. Be good to yourself. Be proud of yourself.

Be ready to put yourself first to fulfill your wants. What does this mean? Do you snub others? Do you disregard their opinions, their wants? Do you not care for them anymore? Au contraire, of course not. It only means that you cannot give up a genuine want because of someone, that you do not claim to like something because it pleases someone. You do not do things because someone demands something that is not satisfying to you.

Strike a balance of being in your centre of power but do not forget others. Be kind to others and they will be kind to you. Be respectful towards others and they will be respectful towards you.

But start with yourself. Be kind to yourself. Be respectful to yourself. All will be returned to you tenfold. Such is the law. Give and you will be given. Ask and you shall receive the answer. Seek and it will be revealed. Such is the law.

The best of all is to come. But do you know that the best of all is here? You are here to unravel the mystery of yourself. You are here by your own choice. You choose where you are. You choose what you do, so choose wisely. Choose out of respect for yourself, and then others. Choose from your heart.

Human beings go on in their lives without stopping and asking, "Is this why I am here? Is this what I came to do?" Stop and ask those questions. Stop and keep on asking. The replies will come to you. Your questions will be answered.

Without the power of being in the centre of one's being, life is lost wandering. It is a life without a goal. It is a life without direction. It is a life without knowing where you want to be. Do you know where you want to be?

Do you know where your heart is leading you? Ask the question. Ask and the answers will be revealed to you.

When you tap into your Being you will know how to, where to, why. You will know that which is for you or not. You will know that you can hurt someone just with words. You will know that kindness is best. You will know that respect is best. You will know that ridicule does not work. Putting out fear does not work. Belligerence does not work. You may get a short bout of satisfaction but in the long run you will receive what you sow. Sow belligerence and you shall receive it in return. Sow contempt and you get that too. Sow joy and smiles, and you get them back.

Getting the picture? Be aware of yourself. Do not walk through your life without a purpose. Take care of your soul and body. Be aware of that which is good for you. Live with intent and calmness will be yours. Quiet, appreciative joy will be yours. The unhurried pace of your life stream will be yours.

Living a purposeful life does not mean that you need to achieve extraordinary things. You do not need to be known and famous in worldly terms, known to others through worldly success. If that is your destiny, so be it. But that is not what we are talking about. Purposeful living is to be and go about your life in a purposeful fashion, with love tending to your garden, if you like gardening. If it is something that you do not enjoy, don't do it. If it is something you enjoy, do it. Find your purpose and do it with love.

Purpose in life is being in the presence of your life. Do not think of lost opportunities. Do not think and worry of your future days. Be in the centre of your power today. Enjoy your day. Be entrenched in your present day. With calm and joy ask your heart to be in the centre of your power today.

If you are centred in today, you will never worry about the future day, as all can only be today. Once you are living it, you will know the difference. Your life will flow and be simplified. You will take care of your day's activities and will not need to worry about tomorrow, because there is no tomorrow. There is always a next day, and each is today. Keep that in mind and be with your heart in the centre of your power.

Do not dwell on your past either. Do release your past as you have done the best you could have. That is why you did what you did. That is what you knew and felt at the time. That is who you were at the time. Bless it and let it go. If you need to, forgive. Forgive yourself and those around you, or those involved, and let go. Then fill the surrendered place with love. Send love to yourself and others and be done with it.

So what is it that you can do? Love yourself, be kind to yourself. Live your daily life as best as you know how. Do not worry about the past or future. Do spend your today anchoring the foundation for tomorrow that will be your today. Do not believe in those who would like to stop you from your own path. Do believe in yourself. After all, if you always consult with your heart and listen to its guidance, you always will be in the centre of your power without hurting yourself or others.

Namaste. We love you and appreciate your attention. Amen.

The direct sponsoring of your thoughts is the prime reason for events to appear in your life. Direct sponsoring means that a direct thought, that is repeated again and again, takes a message to the universe and the universe complies by affording the circumstances to you. Thus, creation comes from you. It is formed at a higher level and comes back to you.

These thoughts of yours need to be consistent to create a certain situation. For instance, if you are in fear and always worry about the state of your financial affairs, you will receive what you worry about—an unstable situation. That is the law. What you fear you attract. What you fear you attract, remember that. That is the nature of your thought. What you think of most of the time will materialize in your life. That is the law.

Do not allow yourself to fear, to loathe. Manage your fears not, and that is what you will attract to yourself. They will appear and test you. Until you understand this, you will create many unpleasant events and sicknesses through your own doing.

You may not like what you read. You may think: "I have been visited by this unpleasant situation that is so painful and is hurting me, and now it appears that I am the one responsible for bringing it into my life."

And that is exactly how it is. You are a creator. You are the maker of your destiny. That is the law. Your thoughts are mirrored in your life. Are you unhappy with your present situation? Do not bring your mind toward it. Tell your mind that all is fine and taken care of and believe that. Be consistent in thinking of positive and happy times. Afford yourself the best thoughts. Afford yourself that which is the purest harmony and calm. Your life will be of the purest harmony and calm.

You must understand that the result may not be seen for a while, but do not give up. Be steady in your thought. You took time to create the present events in your life, and to undo what you have created, you need to be consistent in knowing that your happiness and joy are possible once you decide that is how it is.

Know that you are the creators of your lives. You can change where you are. You can change what you are. You can change how you feel. You can change how and if you react.

You are in the centre of your life. Allow yourself to create your better, more enjoyable life. Do stop consciously and subconsciously creating that which you do not like, that which hinders you and does not serve you. Be in control of your life and create events in your day consciously. Be always ready to see the positive in all that appears in your life. Remember, your thoughts are the prime motives for your events to show up.

But you may say, "And hmm... what about the events that visit my country?" Remember, all events are created by thoughts. It is you and your compatriots that create your country's destiny. Nobody else is responsible for where you are. Are you in an earthquake zone? You don't like it? Well, get going and move. It is as simple as that.

All events in your life have a deeper meaning on the spiritual level that you can unravel if you care to do so. Once you understand this, you can change them. You can change your thoughts, your beliefs. It is you and nobody else who is responsible for all that appears in your life. It is you and nobody else who creates all that which is visited upon you. It is you. Do not create events in your life that hurt or do not serve you. So, what is it going to be? Are you going to imagine you are a victim or a martyr? Do not. You can do better than that and once you understand, you will.

Do not stay in a situation that is not to your liking. Do not be with people that are not to your liking. Be aware of your powerful self. Be aware of your own role in your life. It is you and no one else who influences the outcome of events that come to you.

Keep on working with this principle. Watch yourself. What is it you think of most of the time? Is your mind more often than not saying "Boy, oh boy", or is your mind saying "What a great and beautiful day"? You may be surprised about what you find out. Most of you are not aware of all the negative thoughts passing through your minds. Do not complain, do no argue, do not be obsessed with other people. Understand your own role, as that is the most important influence in your life. Be aware, you are it. You create your life story, so know that which you want to paint on the canvas of your life.

And with that we beg you a nice day. We love you and cherish you. Amen.

Work with your psyche to unravel your origins. Work through prayers, affirmations and meditations. Bring calmness and trust into your environment. Please yourself whenever you feel like pleasing yourself. Be diligent in the support of yourself. Do not expect others to give you that support. Do not expect others to be responsible for you. Do not expect others to look out for you.

You need to drive it all. You are the concern of yourself. You are the subject of your life. You are your own charge. Do not think that anybody in any way is responsible for your upkeep, your enjoyment.

Your own exuberance comes from you. Your own depression comes from you. Your own melodramatics come from you. Your own enthusiasm comes from you. Do you understand? It is you. No one else needs to feed your physical, emotional and spiritual needs. If you are blessed by all that which comes to your life through your own care, you will attract those of the same beliefs and you will be able to rejoice in their company.

Renew your thoughts. Renew your actions. Are you unhappy? Discard that feeling and start fresh. Are you sick? Discard that as well.

Helena, you may say, "Hmm, discard? I myself just now went through a lengthy sickness and took quite an effort to become better."

If you do not see what is coming to you, it can crush you. If you do not see what is bestowed upon you, you will not change it. See what is bestowed upon you by examining yourself, as it is bestowed upon you by you. Be ready to confess to yourself. Be ready to be honest with yourself. Be ready and you will be rewarded.

Seli atu ami no ke leti? Si ma tu ole mo.

By examining and acknowledging all that hinders you, you will make big strides towards enriching your life to one that will become joyful and healthy. You will be more knowing of what to do and where to go. You will be more knowing about you. You will be in charge of you, as that is what you are — you are in charge of yourself.

You need to understand that. Nobody else is charting your course. It is you. You can say, "But, but, this and that happened to me." Really? Did it happen to you, or was it grown out of thoughts and actions you had before?

Believe me, you will find that you can trace all "accidents" to a time when you either thought of them or to when you perhaps went somewhere where you did not want to be, and voila, an accident happened just as the universe fulfilled your wishes.

There is a saying: *boku moir tu li mo. Seti la an thi se me.* We do not intend to translate word for word here. All we can say is that the future is affected by the past and vice versa. All is connected; therefore there is no distinction at all. Such is the force of your thoughts that it prevails in the acts that come to you. You are responsible for all that happens to you. You may not understand this until, by the force of your unhappy and painful experiences, you realize that the maker is you and not somebody outside of you.

If you do not repair all that which ails you within, damage will be shown without. Regardless of how you feel, with the proper attitudes you can derive a lot from your life. Are you sad? Well, get over it. It is your own power that comes into play and changes your attitudes. Are you depressed? Change it. Be not depressed. You can move yourself in and out of feelings and moods. Try it. You will be amazed at the power you have. Without changing the circumstances, you will be in another space.

Understand your own potential. Understand your own power of creation. Understand that you are the god of your own world. So behave like one. Be strongly entrenched in your spiritual self. Be strongly connected with your heart. Be strong in the support of yourself. Be strongly amiable to others. See that you continue on this path and the results will come back to you ten-fold.

Will you be my spiritual guide? Will you be my tutor? Will you be my this and that? These questions need to be answered in the right sequence. At first, you may need outside influences and guidance. At first. But the time will come when none is needed. Your power from within becomes your lighthouse. Your power from within becomes your guiding post.

Will you be my caretaker? Will you be my crutch and helper? Is that how you want to spend your life on Earth? Be all blessed who help others, but remember, you, those who are being helped, the day must come when you stand on your own feet, use your own judgment, are responsible for yourselves.

Do you understand the consequence of you not doing any of this? Can you imagine you coming here again and again, feeling lost? Looking for help? Being in fear? Agonizing over your decisions? Looking for someone to hold your hand again and again?

Of course not. That is not how you want to be and to continue to be. So become self-sufficient and strong to start on the path of recovery of your own self-esteem, your own self-guidance, your own power. Be advised by your heart and you will succeed. We do not promise roses. You need to promise roses to yourself.

This rendering is for those who still do not get that they are responsible for their woes and joys. Those who cannot get it will get it when they are ready to get it. Such is the law. Your own higher self will test you, will prod you, will persuade you, to discover that you, only you, are responsible for you. It is that simple.

And with that, we are signing off. Namaste and sayonara. We love you and cherish you. Amen.

Spirit knows that awakening seems to come from outside influences. Outside influences are catalysts. Nevertheless, if you do not balance the inside influences, then the outside, however forceful or tragic, will not produce a change. Another new experience will need to come to restore the balance.

Once you reach equilibrium, there is the constant desire to keep it. However, in the process of encountering new experiences, the equilibrium shifts and then you again seek recovery. This sea-saw movement produces quality changes. The quantity of quality changes grows, and then you reach a new level of your understanding and knowledge. The long trail of being in the same and same is broken. Your education accelerates. Your masculine and feminine come together. Your spirit is closer to you. It resides within, and it and you, as a carrier of that within, are in tune. This state produces euphoria, a blissful state of being when the balance of spiritual and other bodies is in synch.

Ristu mali nu? Eti ti pa ti le? Der mi na lu a? Sali tila meli nu. Eski tu? Sali mile numi tu. Eti la mi no. Resti pa amino nati ly omi. Deli ca to mi nu at i suli ki.

The power of creation is in all of you. The power of knowing is in all of you. There is a power within that connects without. This power, if recognized, will advance you toward the realization of your latent potentials.

La ti mi nu? Et ti ku? Sel ami notila. Boti kuli ma.

Anomaly is when you are not in touch with your powerful self. Anomaly is when you think that you are powerless and strewn around by outer influences. Anomaly is when you think that your voice does not count. Anomaly is to not be in the centre of your power. Be powerful and you will move mountains. All the molehills will evaporate and the big hindrances will become smaller. By realizing your own power, the change your creative self can accomplish, if deciding to do so, is enormous.

Be aware of your power. Every day do realize it and do something you have never done before. Power. Be powerful. Come to those who snub you and show that of yourself which is forgiving and inviting. Come to your family and show them that of yourself which is driven by the heart. Come to your enemies and start a dialogue from your heart knowing how powerful you are. Come to those you never went to and help them on their own path of being powerful.

Take your health, your riches into your own hands. Know that your abundance has no limits. Do not limit yourself by anything or anybody. Come to your Mother-Father God not as a beggar or whiner, but as an equal member of the same family of creation of those who are created in God's image.

Staying in your true power, being from your heart is where you need to be. Powerful without heart is not what you want to be. And that is how most are. Powerful, regardless of what it costs them or others. Therefore, ego driven power, no; heart driven power, yes!

And that is all for now. Have a great day. We love you and we cherish you.

Thank you.

Chapter Seven

The Choices Are Yours

Laissez passer. "Laissez passer" is the motto of those who know. They know that those who are set in their ways do not want to be corrected. They need to become aware on their own. When their realization becomes complete, they will correct their ways in the most appropriate manner for them. Laissez passer is the way of letting them come to their own conclusions. Such is the nature of humanity. No pushing or prodding is adequate in terms of learning. All that they do is of their own accord. This does not discount the need for teachers and guidance, however. Once a person becomes aware of his or her fallibility and decides to change, he may seek those who will guide him.

Este mi na to? Del ca ny is.

Your make-up of spiritual, rhetoric, promises, and so on is a delicately weaved web. It is a fragile scenario that is breakable, and it is you who does the breaking. Once you fix the breakages, the path becomes clear.

Na to ami na to. Bi tu oki so.

During the crisis of indecision, during the crisis of inactivity, your psyche undergoes an element of recognition that the way you are at the present stage does not work. Once this insight is there, a period then follows when you may mingle with this thought without doing anything about it. Or, you may act right away. In any case, once you are fed up with your inactivity, you can either forget your dilemma or change it into a non-dilemma. You decide to change, you decide to mend.

Salvation, as an act of God's mercy, does not exist in the sense it is portrayed on Earth. Salvation starts with you. You decide to correct, you decide to add or subtract. Once the possibility of your staying with your decision is evident, the universe takes notice. Once it is certain that you have staying power, the universe delivers. Thus the power of your decision comes into play. No one else can change your own situation. Unless you are ready to change and take that step in your mind, the universe will not provide any clues. Unless you provoke it, it will not remember you.

Always ask for assistance. Always ask questions. Always ask for that which you require. Be consistent in asking, without wavering. Eventually, when it is clear that you are sincere in desiring some situation, it will arrive. Such is the power of concentration. Such is the power of focusing on the subject of your love. Love what you do and you will succeed. Love what you do. If you do not, the energy dissipates. The energy evaporates. That is how it is all the time. Anything that is not of your interest and focus is not supported enough and will disappear.

It is always the same. Your consistency, your true love and dedication to the cause for which you are working is a must. It is a must until you succeed. That is how growth is accomplished. That is how acceleration occurs.

At a certain point, the vibration surge overtakes you and you take a conscious leap. This is a so-called qualitative step, or jump, if you wish.

So, the choices are yours. The choices are not given but taken. You choose which way you go. You choose which way you continue to go.

Your choices do not bind you to anything. You are always free to make changes. If you think that your choice does not serve you any more, make another.

This is applicable to all in your life. Your partners, your homes, your relationships of any kind. There can be changes to your satisfaction at any time. That is what you do when they do not fulfil you anymore. Change your reality and you will have new events in your life. Change the events and you will have a new reality.

All is connected. All is one. Therefore, by choosing a new reality you do not become disjointed from the one you experienced before. You only modify your feelings toward it and from your new point of view, from your new perception, you see and experience it differently. You believe that the change is real.

But what is real? That which you see are just ideas. Ideas of yourself and others materialized into shapes, bodies, sky, skyscrapers. All that you see is chimerical. It is maya, an illusion. If there are enough of consistent thoughts, they bind the formless into solid matter. That is how your reality is created. It is chimerical, it is not real. It is your reality based on your thoughts. The solidity is your perception. It is not there. It is a perception of yours that keeps you in your belief that all seen and touched around you is as solid as a rock. There is nothing further from the truth. All is manageable if you know how.

You can pass through your solid matter without any problems. You can pass through anything on your planet. As that is what you see, a passable, chimerical material that only appears to be solid.

That is all for today. Amen and namaste. We love you and we cherish you. Bye.

During your life journey, you will meet many. You will discover that many will pass by you without any notice and many will be with you as your true friends and acquaintances. Why is that? Is it that you have links from other lifetimes? Is it that you need to stick together and make the best of your lives on Earth? Is it both?

You may be kindred souls of the same origin. You may have lived many times as sister and brother, father or mother. You may be soul mates who are coming together this time.

Yesterday you were not the person that you are today. Tomorrow you will be a different person than you are today. Such is the pace of evolution that nothing is static, nothing is repeated. As one snowflake is different from another, the same are your lives—different every time you materialize on this plane. Differences breed different experiences, and you will learn all that is necessary to open your path toward understanding your origins.

Your inquisitive nature asks, "Where and how can I find who I am?" Well, do not look to us. Look toward where you are, toward yourself. Misinterpretation is if you think that the full understanding of your life comes from the outside. That is not something that can give you an explanation of your life. Treat yourself to many sources of information and you will be puzzled. Treat yourself to only one—your own, your own counsel, your own guidance—and you will have one infallible source of information that is directly linked to your God and Goddess.

Be ready to screen any other opinions that people around you give you, as that is their observation. You need your own observation to come to you. That is the only one that is valid for you. No other person can supply the wisdom. Only you can shed wisdom on you. That is the law.

Understand that this does not mean that nobody else can have a valid opinion. Rather, if you are seeking a full-blown explanation of yourself, do not look to others. It is only you who can understand you. Any outside help is simply a crutch. That crutch is not what you need. That crutch is only good for a while, until you stand on your own two feet, firmly entrenched. Then you take your own steps. Then you rely on your own strength.

Understand? You are a pillar of wisdom and knowledge to yourself. Anything else is a crutch that is good only until you are firmly rooted in you. And that is what you need to understand. That is what comes to play in all scenarios of your lives.

It is not only wisdom you are seeking. Relying on your strength also predisposes how you feel, how vital and healthy you are. Do not look to get healthy from other people. You decide that health is your priority and then act on it. Believe that you are healthy, and your health will materialize.

Do not be inclined to seek help from others, as that is a way of prolonging dependency. Of course you may say, "I tried that and I could not get the result I was asking for". Yes, it does take mastering. The main point is for you to trust that you are creator. You are the one to help you. Ask and it will be given to you. Believe and trust that the deed is already done and the universe will deliver.

Do not prolong your suffering by running around looking for outside influences. Be ready to approve of yourself. Be ready to help yourself. Be ready to stand on your own two feet. Be ready to be your own boss, you own god, as that is who you are. Discover that which is your inherent right and gift from your supreme creator. You all are offspring of God; you were made in his image.

Helena, we would like you take a rest.

I feel tired today but I can still continue.

Your tiredness steeps from your disbelief that you are well. Trust is needed and the healing will complete itself without any outside influences.

And with that, namaste and sayonara. We love you and cherish you. Be well, and be ready to approve of yourself. Amen.

Mais oui, mais oui,
here we come again.
We are following your thought train.

We are following it
and we want to let you know
that your willingness to cooperate
is bringing results
that will help you grow.

We are happy to let you know
that the Federation of Peace is back.
We are happy to let you know
that you are their target,
target of their transmission.

During the journey on the Earth
millions mill around.
Millions are ready to ask questions
about their spirit
and their mind.

These sessions explain
that which you want to know.
These sessions lead you to get
the picture straight.

These sessions let you understand
how it is that the influences
from below and above
are guiding your life and your love.

Mais oui, mais oui, here we are again.
Mais oui, mais oui, we are attached
to your thought train.
Mais oui, mais oui, here we are.

Dear Helena, this was our plan:
we'd talk and you'd listen.
It is as easy as that,
and we also are listening
to your thought.

We are here to replenish your energy.
Sit straight and receive.
Sit straight and do not type.
We are here to send you light.
Light, that will open your chakras
to the reception of the highest order
of pure light and unconditional love.

Mais oui, mais oui, here we are again,
attached to your thought train.
Mais oui, mais oui.

Unnatural, as it may seem,
are the cravings
for abundance and for sweets,
for all good things.
Unnatural, as it may seem,
the poverty image seems to prevail.

Unnatural, as it may seem,
is the uncertainty about which is right.

Is it the poor image or is it abundance? Is it that or the other?

The reply may seem simplistic: it is what you choose. If you choose to live in poverty, that is your highest choice. If you choose to be in abundance, that is your highest choice. It needs then to be adhered to, it needs to be acclaimed. It needs to be proclaimed in every step of your life. If you choose one, then stick with it. Do not wonder if that is the right way to be. Once you decide that that is what you want, it becomes the right way to live. Being poor is fine, if that is what you want. Being abundant if fine, if that is what you want. Live your choice and be happy.

Now listen to this: you can always change your choice. If you find that it does not agree with you anymore or that there is a need to try something else, release the previous choice and choose the new needed choice. You will smoothly flow from one choice to the other.

Remember, choose and adhere to it. If after a time of adherence you learn what you needed from your choice, then you may decide to change and live that new choice. Do not wonder what is right. You, as your own director of your own show decide which way to go. Then stick to it. If it feels good, stay in it. If it feels unpleasant or disagreeable, forget it.

What does this say to you? First, you need to be clear about what you want. You need to know where you want to be.

Do you want to be there or somewhere else? Do you need to be poor or abundant? If the choice is clear, then stick to it. Your perseverance will bring the desired results and will accomplish what you want to accomplish.

All those choices, all those life experiences are needed for you to continue towards the realization that you, as a creator, can make any choice be your choice. So choose and be well acquainted with your wants.

Da re mi su oki no? Seti la seti la? Ami no meneku it. Dere manoi ako ti pu se? Seti la seti la seti la. Mini oke mane to lu seti la seti la. Oka tela meni tosh seti la seti la seti la. A ko set mo ne apo la ti kule omi no te suri mo. Seti la seti la seti la. A ko ste mani la. Tu li ome toru pe. Seti la seti la seti la. Dere omi no. Dere seti la. Dere dere. Ome no. Pati oke se. Tere mino omino ke tu le mi nore o. Seti la seti la seti la. Oke moeno seti la oke po. La.

Bist oke mon la. Seti ro pe ako te. Seti la ome nola dori to seti la kato meni duri ot.

That is all for today, be well. We love you and we cherish you. Amen.

Mani oli tu? Seti la? Emi noli kuti ome nori tula ope la. Seti la seti la seti la. Duli ma noe. Seti la. Duli ma oi ema ni toe. Suti ole k tula oma noti me. Seti la seti la seti la ote mo ne ami no seti la oti mone oke ti. Seti la. Omi nole omi nole. Dera ti mole seti la.

The above says that the wealth of your being is directly proportional to your degree of spirituality. Wealth itself is deceiving. It is not so much a measurement as it is a practiced thing to be given or taken to or from those who do not deal with their needs and wants appropriately. This is not to say that those in need will receive. To the contrary, being in need is not the way. Being in need is the way to the poor house.

Being in wealth, being in riches is the way to riches. Contradictory statement? Not at all. Rich thinking leads to riches. Poor thinking leads to the poor house. This is a fact. If you have a dime, behave as though it is a dollar.

If you have a dollar, behave as though it is a ten-dollar bill. Be ready to raise it tenfold. Be ready to imagine it being tenfold. And tenfold it will become.

Seti la seti la is the way to come to your God. Call him. Call your Mother and Father. Your God will reply. Call, ask and you will receive. Be ready to receive and you will receive. Be ready not to receive and you will not. Trust and you will be trusted.

When you appreciate yourself, when you love yourself, when you are in gratitude to yourself, you are ready to receive. Only in your worthy, appreciative state of yourself, you are ready to receive. Blissful is the way for those who know themselves and appreciate themselves for what they are. Blissful is their way. Toward the creator within they go. They go with their own rhythm of their being.

Be ready to receive. That is all you need to do. Be ready to receive. Every minute of your life, be ready. Be ready, be ready, be ready. *Seti la seti la seti la*. Be ready.

Dimly lit is the colour of human needs. Humans are not too perceptive of their own wants. Humans are not perceptive of their own desires. They casually remark that this and that is needed, however, there is no follow up. This stagnation in the process of acquisitions leads to problems with the results. Stagnation is typical of all, no matter what gender, political or religious, or other affiliation. There is a void in understanding that anything, and we repeat, anything, can be yours if properly asked for.

How do you ask to cover your desires? It is the honour of the universe to supply and it always does. Inasmuch we know, that is how it always works. Inasmuch you do not know, it always works. All you need to do is to ask. Ask and it will be given to you. Ask and you shall inherit the Earth. Ask and you will be supplied. Ask, believe and receive.

Ask for what your wants are coaching you to ask for.

Then you wait?

No. Then assume that you already have it.

And assume that you already have it until you have it?

Yes, certainly. That is how it is. Assume that you have already received your goods. Assume that you already have them. Assume that you are already using them. Assume that your life is abundant, including all that you asked for. You already have it. Do you understand? Assume your possession right away and have no doubt that you will possess.

This is how it works. Imagine that you want more money, that you have a certain amount every month. Imagine how it feels; with passion imagine your abundance. Trust; believe and know that it has always been yours. Articulate it through your knowingness, through your true belief. And when you know of it, then it is. That is how it works.

Always be thankful and grateful for all that you have. Always know that you are worthy of what you have and what you ask for. Always assume that you have already received your wish. Assume, assume, assume that you already have it, that right away you have it. Assume until it arrives and it is yours forever.

Then you make another wish. Simple, right?

Yes, it sounds simple. Why have I not thought of it?

Because you are worried about not having what you want to have, that you don't have time to take a proper stand and acquire your want. Waiting for your goods to appear slows everything down. Assuming that you have them is the way to go.

Do not say, "I don't trust, I need to see it. Until I see it I cannot have it." You do have it at all times, because it is already there, it is always there. All you need to do is assume your possession and it will materialize at your doorstep, so to speak. Keep at it and it will come.

Such is the power of asking, imagining, feeling and knowing that you have already received everything you want.

Namaste and sayonara from your friends of the Universal Consciousness. Amen.

Thank you for coming.

We are happy to come every time you need us, just call.

Dula mu ti alo. Seti la, seti la. Meti no mi o. Seti la. Seti la. Meni o, meni o.

Seti la. Seti la. Seti la. Seti la. Ami no meni to seru mino ku. Ati meno ti sa le ma o. Peru mu ano minako. Seti la. Seti la seti la. Seti la amona se la. Seti la amo na sela. Seti la amo na se la e seti la amo na se la. Ruti o mana ku je mi no seti la.

A si tu elo me natusi e mi na. Seti la seti la. Meni su amo ni. Seu ma ti ke mo ni seti la. Seti la seti la seti la seti la, amo na kur ri la seti la seti la. Amo ni menu si, amo ni menu si, menu si amo ni seti la seti la. Amo ni seti la amo ni seti la amo ni seti ru ku ri la seti la. Amo ni seti la amo ni seti la kuri mu seti la amo ni seti la. Seti la. Seti la …

Best of all is here, sing it our dear... best of all is here, sing our dear...

Seti la seti la amo nu ku rila seti la seti la amo ni ku rila. Seti la seti la seti la seti la. A moni moni la.

There is a rhythm in life. There is a rhythm in everything. When you find that rhythm, it influences you as you go on. When you find your rhythm, you can dance to it. When you find your rhythm, you can sing to it.

Seti la seti la seti la seti la seti la seti la seti la seti la.

Rhythm is here, rhythm is here, rhythm is here. *Seti la seti la seti la seti la seti la seti la seti la oh oh seti la.*

Sing more. You will be joyful because your heart will sing. *Seti la seti la seti la seti la seti la seti la.*

Your higher self knows where to spot you; it is in touch with you at all times. It knows about you, so it can test you and design for you a testing ground, and yet another and another, where you go and experience hardship and joy, where you experience disharmony and harmony. Where you know that to be in harmony is better than being in disharmony.

Of course, this is not so clear when you do not know that you are not in harmony, that you are disharmonic. Sometimes you do not know until it is so painful that you need to break away from your pain. Sometimes the pain is so big and so unbearable that then, and only then, can you come to realize the foolishness of your ways. Then you come to realize that you can change where you are, what you do.

You do not need to wait for a change. You do that change yourself. You change whenever you need to because all was created by you in the first place. That is the rule. You are the facilitator of changes. You create and you recreate. You change and build again. You do the living. You do the changing. You are the one who is compelled to continue no matter how you feel, because to stay where you are, because to stagnate, is not to live.

You need to live. You need to prosper. You need to progress. You need to go on. You need to awaken. You will and you are doing this already. You will go on until you reach the full realization of your potential, of your original self.

You cannot avoid the changes, no matter how much you want to postpone them. Because you are afraid. Because you do not know what will happen. Because you cannot see where it will lead you. Because you are uncomfortable with the changes. Because you are comfortable. Because you are set in your ways. Because you are used to it. You are used to being where you are. It does not matter how painful it is or not. You are used to it and it is familiar.

So, what is it going to be? Familiarity or progress? Do you know what you want? Do you know where to go? Remember to ask your heart. "My heart, do you like where you are? Do you like what you do? Do you like what is dished out to you?" And then listen. Listen with care. What is it your heart is telling you? What is it your heart is asking you to do? Are you listening? Listen, and act in accordance with what you hear, as that is the only way to live.

Must you continue? Nobody must do anything. Why the compelling feeling then? Because you are driven to it by not liking where you are. You need change. You are heeding the call of your higher self. Your higher self is calling you, is showing you the way. It wants you to evolve and come back home. Realize that. This is not your home, however comfortable you feel. Your home is where the spirit roams, where the consciousness is free. Where the spirit is free to roll over and say, whoa, I love where I am, no dense physical body for me anymore.

Read this and realize that you are welcome to come home any time. Who is holding you back? Yourself. Who is not allowing you to come here? Yourself. Who is not telling you that you can go at any time, any time at all? Yourself.

Because of what? Because of fear of change. Because of feeling comfortable and settled down. Because you know where you are and you fear that which you do not know. But do you not know it? No, you know. You know everything. You know it. Let yourself recall that part of you. Remember yourself. Remember your origins. Remember your life as a free consciousness, roaming without restraints and feeling limitless.

Don't you wish you were like that again? Don't you wish to feel that freedom again? Don't you wish to join us again? Do you not? That feeling is ingrained deep within you. That feeling has been and always will be there.

If you know it or not, you belong here. Ultimately you will come back. It only depends on you how fast you understand and decide that yes, now I am done here and I do not want to be here anymore.

And that is how it is. You decide. Nobody else decides for you. You will come, as nobody will bring you. You will come and we will greet you all. We will handle you gently. We will show you around. We will help you remember. We will come with you anywhere you want us to go.

And that is what we do. We are the angels. We are the helpers. We are the facilitators. We are the advisors.

We are the guides. We are your charges. You can ask us anything, and we will facilitate that it comes to you.

This is a promise. So be well and work on your re-membrance. Be well and enjoy your life wherever you are, at whatever point of your life you are. We are with you. We are your helpers. And we are waiting patiently for your awakening.

Namaste and sayonara. We love you and cherish you. Amen. Good night.

Thank you. Good night.

Chapter Eight

You Are Supported by Many

Deri mela tuli po ana me ti ku? Seti la seti la. A ko meni puli sa seti seti la.

During a crisis of the body and mind, the spirit hovers around, supporting the structure. During such a time, many see the light in a delusionary flight from their bodies as the spirit takes them to their original self, the pure consciousness.

This state is debated by the medical profession, which works on proofs. Proof is that we are connected, such as with this writer. Proof is that we are hovering around Helena, such as now. None of this is 3-D proof. However, that is as far as we can prove it. So what is it you can do? Nothing too much. Apart from your faith and trust, there is no hard evidence. Such is the story of Daniel in the Lion's Den, such are stories of ancient times. None of these are provable, yet you still like to read them. So, why don't you listen to this story?

Eons ago, (this is not provable, remember?) the Earth was not, God was not, the universe was not. Consciousness was. It was churning and churning on its own and was not all that certain where to go. Certainty was not a virtue that it possessed. It came up with the idea of expanding its churning little dot into a bigger dot. Then it expanded further and created and created. All that is, is a result of this creation. And so God became.

God became? How?

Well, he always was. He came to be God when you started calling him God. That consciousness is God, God is that consciousness. That consciousness that flows through all, that intelligence which flows through all in its purest form is you, and just allowing this thought enhances your connection with God. Connect with that thought. Connect and be comfortable with the thought that this godly power, or consciousness, pervades each of your cells, every cell of every individual, every cell and molecule of that which is visible and not. There is no other way, as all has consciousness in itself, all is consciousness.

There is a way of contacting this consciousness, if you quiet yourself down. If you stop thinking and just be. If you keep on practicing this, you will start hearing the "conversations" of those around you, such as those of the nature spirits and your body elementals serving you. Those of your bed and your chair serving you.

Did you know that you have always been fully served and supported by many? Did you know that you are their object of adoration? Did you know that you need to return that love they have for you?

Why don't you then give them your love back? Why don't you tell them how you appreciate the services and support they give you? Why don't you get in touch with them? Tell your body, tell your cells how you appreciate them. Tell your old trusty furniture how you love it. Tell all those around you how you like them and how you know that they are the best for you. Tell all about your love and support for them. Tell them at all times and love them back. Support them, show them your appreciation.

And that is how you connect. Through love vibrations you connect with others. Through these vibrations you feel their joys and pains. Through these vibrations you come to the realization how connected you all are. You all are throbbing in a similar rhythm. You all are asking similar questions. You all are looking for the same answers. You all are. Consciously realize the fact that through your love for each other, you can connect and be one.

Amen. Thank you for coming this morning.

You are welcome.

Be back.

Yes, I will.

That is all for now. We love you and we cherish you. Amen.

Deli ka ti mi? Suti li? Amo sila meni?

Esti mu nila? Eti pi limo? Deti ola tuli po? Seti la? Seti la. Deli kati mu ti o. Peri situ ma li no. Esti ola ditu me. Aki muni tu la se. Delti delti omi ko. Seti ama tomiko. Esti la esti la do ti.

Destitute are those who cannot find peace. Destitution, it may seem, is many people's fate. Destitute, it may seem, are the lives of many people. It is not a mark of physical unhappiness. It is the mark of a message coming from your higher self: "I am calling you and I need you to acknowledge me. I am calling you, as this is where you exist. I am calling you, as it is time for you to reconnect."

The destitute feeling of being abandoned stems from not being in touch with your higher self, with your spiritual self. Destitution is not something you will experience if your being is ingrained in your spiritual self. It is an illusion that exists if you do not know from where you came and seek without any clues.

The destitute feeling of being abandoned is sometimes all that is needed for people to snap and start looking for solutions. It is often a springboard to looking into the depths of their being. It is stepping down, down, down, onto the last rung of a long ladder, where a personal hell is reached, and where the only way to continue is to start climbing up.

Do not be in or remain in destitution. It needs to come to an end. Destitution is a state of mind when all hope is gone, when trust is no longer there, when one's real feelings are suppressed, when the soul feels barren, when the messiah does not come. Destitution clouds your mind and does not allow you to see properly. When in the grips of destitution, the destitute person does not follow through with their own intuition, through their own premonitions.

Once they realize this, the power of restoration surges forward with conviction and establishes a rapport between the destitute one and her higher self. This progress can be painful and may be hindered by a feeling of being alone.

This process is not something that you would like to cancel, for when destitution eats at the fabric of one's life

it may end in suicide. Because of the love for one's freedom, a destitute person may be ready to end all their
hindrances at once in order to shake off the shackles of
their oppressive situation. Such is a destitute person's
will that it sometimes does not matter to them whether
they live or die.

Destitution will grip you until you decide that that's
it, no more of this. No more of these destitute feelings.
No more of this destitute crying. No more. Step out and
grab that which is You out there, waiting for you to connect. Step out of your misery and ask for that piece of
you that is yours to connect with. Allow joy and happiness to come into your life.

Destitution serves as a condition that brings many
other destitute people to rally around the one who is as
destitute as they. By coming together and deciding to
clear their feelings, they can bring joy back to themselves
through the realization that beyond here is where they
are, and that there is more.

There is more. There are vast fields of many options,
of many probabilities, of many different existences. And
not only that, there are levels existing within levels
where all is expanded into innumerable and immeasur-
able possibilities.

Then what is actually there? This is what everybody
wants to know. Sometimes we do not even know. Such is
the vastness of the universes created by God. God, or
whomever you see in his or her place. God, as a multi-
dimensional creator, a supreme being of supreme consciousness, who is controlling not, unfriendly not. Who
is pure love. Pure energy and light.

Where does he reside? Everywhere. Where is his throne, his very own place? Everywhere. He is nowhere and everywhere. He just is. His place is within your hearts. His place is within your bodies. His place is within a tree, a deer. He is. She is. She is a queen who is not in charge by power and suppression but by love and immense understanding. He is your Father, she is your Mother. He, as a Father, is loving. He does not preach. His ways are her ways. Her ways are his ways. They are one and will never be separated. Creation is without separation. From one to another, ideas flow. From one to another, events flow. From one to another, actions flow.

This is an attempt to explain unconditional love and acceptance, and the feeling of belonging that you can have when you live in the flow of love. In the feeling of love, there is no death, there is no sorrow, there is no unhappiness. In this form, beings can flow from one to another in total understanding and acceptance. The viable source of unconditional love is the creator's heart, God and Goddess in one.

That is all for now. We love you and we cherish you. Amen.

You may ask, "But once I am destitute, how do I deal with it?" Do not deal with "it". Deal with yourself. Deal with your mind playing tricks on you. Deal with that portion of you that is your personality and ego, which clings to the belief that once you see that their ways do not serve, once you see through their games, you will abandon them.

Your ego and personality are your co-travelers. You are their boss, but at the same time, they control you, they move you left and right.

How? You listen to their tastes and wants. You are driven by them. They guide you to satisfy them. If you satisfy them, they feel good. And, as you associate with them, you feel good. They cannot be without you, so they want you to think that you are them. They want you to think that you are one. You need to understand that you, a divine being, are not them.

We would like you to ponder this: your ego and personality are the main characteristics of your life on Earth. You can change them, but they are strongly entrenched in you and you will need a lot of willpower to move and change them. They need you; therefore, they are inclined to cooperate. If you work with them, you will all grow together until ego and personality are no longer separate from you and you all blend. You all benefit from the change—you, your ego and personality. Then you move on, you graduate.

> *I am not quite clear on how this all works. For in-stance, when we leave Earth, what happens to ego and personality? Do they merge with us or are they discarded? Do they become integrated with us, does their integration happen once we move on from this planet; does integration ever happen? Please explain further.*

What happens is that ego and personality, being a product of human lives, eventually get integrated into your psyche. Once you understand the life you lead on Earth, you will know how to be in your divinity. You will use your Earthly vices to your advantage and will utilize and include them in your divine self.

This will be the next evolutionary step. Your psyche will deal with the likes of your ego and personality in such a way that it will re-educate them to the point where the differences between your divine and the rest of your Earthly characteristics no longer exist. You will then explore the integration of both into your element of divine psyche. When this happens, ego and personality lose their 3-D upbringing and are absorbed by your divinity.

How would you characterize ego and personality?

You live behind a veil; you are veiled from knowing your true self. You need to rediscover and experience your divine roots. You must peel away all the layers acquired by reincarnating on Earth. The common thread is the ego and personality that bind the structures together.

How do they bind and what structures?

The mind and psyche bridge the gap between the known and unknown. Psyche is that part of you which talks to your divinity. Mind talks to psyche. There is a hierarchy in everything, without which the processes would not flow. Jumping from one state to another would lead to confusion. You developed these structures through the evolution of the human race. The hierarchy of systems and functions was established and that is where ego and personality fit.

It is like this: your mind is influenced by your ego and personality. Your psyche is not in direct contact with the ego and personality. The contact is through the mind. Your mind talks to your ego and personality, then to your psyche. Your psyche then contacts your divine. These are the processes that have evolved since humanity began inhabiting the planet Earth. The conduit has been established and you are just using it without understanding it fully.

Your divine is not entirely plausibly visible on Earth. Only through your mind, your psyche, can glimpses of your divinity be seen. As we said, through your psyche you reach your divine. Through your ego and personality, you reach your mind. Your mind is in contact with your psyche. Therefore, the stage is set and the divine mind is misrepresented by ego.

We would like to clarify the following: you, as a conduit to us, are talking through your divine, your I Am, to us. The process is similar, as described before.

Your higher self directs your psyche. Then the psyche talks to your mind. Your mind arranges the translation from the vibrations it receives via the psyche, and all is translated into words that represent our vibrational input to your divine. Are we making it clear?

> Yes. And how do ego and personality come into the picture?

You transcribe what you hear. By doing that, you involve your ego and personality. Your personality is delighted, as it is an interesting project for it. Your ego is delighted, as it feels important. Do not misunderstand. What we mean is that they both are pleased. Your ego and personality are pleased, and accept that this is where you are.

We would like to explain further, how you, as in humanity, function.

First, you were born. Then you were educated by parents, family, school, friends, society, etc. You developed certain habits and likes or dislikes. You developed your personality, which started splitting from you, your true self, and started living its own life. The same process happened with your ego. These two impostors of your real self then started running your life through commanding what you needed, you liked or not.

You started associating yourself with your needs, likes and dislikes and the pretenders became more and more entrenched in your real self. These two pretenders are parading as though they are you. They became you, as far as they and you are concerned.

Disassociation from them occurs when you start to understand that the real you is not your ego and personality. When that happens, you can literally obliterate them and live as your real self. However, most of you take a different route. You work on mellowing them and on integrating them into the process of your psyche and your divine. All become one.

As we said, you most likely do not discard them. If you do and are not fully aware, exhibiting your divine self, this process becomes very traumatic and you may fall ill, both mentally and physically. Therefore, for most of you, the easiest process is incorporating yourself into them, or rather, them into you. When that happens, you do not need to separate yourself from them. They become you and will serve you on a much higher level than before. The ego will not be an altered ego, which is self-centered and easily hurt. Your personality will exhibit the virtuous qualities of a realized human being.

Is this becoming clearer?

Perhaps. If there is more information, please add.

Yes. There is always more. Information is inexhaustible.

We wish for you to know the following: your ego may be so strong that your pangs of anxiety will not go away until you realize that you can actually talk to your ego. Say, "My ego, why are you so hurt? If you are hurt, it hurts me as well. I would like you to feel that you always have my support. I always support you, as I value you in my life. I value your contribution to who I am." If you do this, your ego will mature from a little whiny child, and you will start supporting and understanding each other better.

Once you support your ego, there will be no limit to how it can support you. Your ego will be ready to stand by you and will not feel threatened by other egos or humans. It will know that whatever happens, you are strongly behind it, and with your guidance, it will grow to become one with you. You will not need to separate from each other when you leave this planet, and your ego will come to its own understanding of the divine nature of all things.

Thank you. How about personality? What is personality? How does it differ from ego?

Ego and personality do not understand your divinity. They do not see your connection to your creator and your higher self. They only operate on the 3-D level and are not worried about anything else but their own survival. They only understand what they see on your planet. Therefore, it is rather difficult to get them to go in the right direction and start recognizing the divinity of yours. They know that they cannot live apart from you, but they do not see your link to your higher self. We would like to add that ego and personality are features of yours that were not discovered until fairly recently, in the late 1800's.

Your personality is about your behaviour qualities, such as your being extroverted or introverted, and the characteristics and identity that people see when they interface with you. Personality is expressed through patterns and behaviours in your physical and mental activities and attitudes.

Ego is more about promoting yourself, about your satisfaction. Your satisfaction is steeped in your ego. You have come to associate yourself with your ego. Your ego is not who you really are. Your ego allows you to imagine that you are separate from the rest of humanity, but know that you all are one.

We would like you to exercise the following: anytime you feel slighted, anytime you feel hurt, stop before you act. Stop and think: "Why is it I feel like this? Why is it that I want to react like this?" And then realize that by changing your feeling about it, you can change the entire situation. Then say: "See, my ego, we changed the situation and you and I, we do not need to feel hurt. In each situation like this I will take care of you."

This will teach your ego that you are the one who runs the show. You are in charge, and you are not swayed by your outer feelings and regrets. You only respond to you inner knowing.

Know that you are linked to your creator, and the outer needs come into balance with the inner. By bringing the inner outward, you will reach that balance. You teaching your ego about your leadership will help to overcome its influence on you. Your personality will follow suit because it is shaped by your ego demands.

And with that, we would like to sign off. Namaste and sayonara. We love you and we cherish you. Amen.

Assure all parts of your being that they are cherished and needed. Assure them that all have their rightful place and need to work together. Assure them of their important roles and let them know that you love and support them. Let them know of your love for them. Let them know of their importance to you. Then let them know that you are their leader, that you are the manager of all of them. Let them know that you, as their leader, are determined to look after them.

By understanding how your mind and body work, you can achieve miracles. You can achieve nirvana. You can reach your potential, which is living your spiritual self here on Earth.

Therefore, treat your body right. Feed it the right food. Do not overindulge. Do not feed your body any food that is devoid of nutrients, that is alcoholic. Do not smoke to hurt your lungs. Sleep enough to allow your body and soul to regenerate. Do not short-change any of your body parts. Exercise and lead a balanced life between your work and family responsibilities, your recreation and rejuvenation.

Does this sound like a tall order? Perhaps. Perhaps for those who are not accustomed to such a way of living. But it is necessary. You need to bring clarity to your lives. Clarity that you, as the boss and caretaker of your body, are in charge and feed it and take care of it in the most appropriate way.

And then, there is your mind. Attend to your mind. Do not leave your mind running constantly. Bringing and running scenarios. Staying in the past. Thinking of the future. Ceaselessly, continually running scenarios. Do not let your mind do that to you. Remember? You are the one who is the boss, so act like one.

Say, "Mind, take a rest. Do not run in a circle. Take a rest, and when I need you, I will call you. Do stay in the present right now. Do stay in this day, do stay in this minute. Attend to that which is the present, attend to that which is now." Keep doing that until you train your mind to obey you and to know that you, as its boss, know when to engage it.

Do not allow your mind to run wild and your body and mind will work together. They will serve you as much as they can. They will respect you. Attend to your body and mind. Love and respect them, and cherish them for what they do for you. They sustain you here on your planet Earth. They offer you a cocoon for your consciousness, your real you. They provide you with a warm and comfortable shelter, which, when taken care of, loved and gently guided, will serve you for many years of mindful life on Earth, where your wisdom will help others.

Have we made this clear? Step into your own power. Do not let your body and mind run you. Let them know that you are the boss. You take care of them so they can take care of you. You decide how and when you will use them. You give them all they require, you feed them the best. You treat them the best. You give them respect at all times and thank them for serving so faithfully.

And this concludes this transcription. The writer needs to go attend to her Tai Chi class. Helena, please come back today. Regenerate and come back.

Yes, I will. Thank you.

Chapter Nine

You Are Connected to Your Source

The power of a spiritual uprising can turn the Earth's massive population around to stand for their rights in a peaceful way. Such is the power of the conviction of your ideas coming from the centre of your empowered self.

Your empowered self is a direct link to the Source. The Source is all empowering, is all encompassing—and what better ally than the Source? There is no better ally than your Source, God and Goddess of your being.

With this, the message is clear. Consult your Source.

You may ask, "And how do I do that?"

Do it with a mind that is set on results.

Say, "I am expecting such and such result... I have a clear picture of it in my mind", and say what it is. Then say "I am expecting it within this time. I thank you for supplying me with this and that... "

Your I Am is always ready to work on your behalf. Your I Am is ready to step in and make sure that the goods are delivered.

You may say, "Hmm, and that seems so easy".

It is, once you are convinced that it is so. You may not be able to deliver at the beginning, but once you stay in the feeling of trust and know that you are looked after, that your Source knows about you, you will receive what you asked for.

Be specific about what you ask for. Nebulous requests are hard to fulfill. Nebulous thoughts can bring surprising results that may not always be pleasant. Many make this discovery and then disbelief sets in.

Always believe that your spiritual link to your Source is open. It is your lifeline. None of the 3-D comforts can uphold you. You are always connected to your Source. You are always energetically supported. Visible not to your eyes, to your senses, it is always there. This is sustenance you can never do without.

Desi tu me? Alo veku? Desi tu la? Ako le mi? Deli tu ma oki la. Re tu oli situ la. Menti oka limi nato. Deli ako seti lumi. Del a ki tu? Seti lumi na.

Best ti ku mi oti so. Re ti tuli omi so. Delti oki. Sa ti mu. Delti oki semi nu. Delti oki suti la. Delti oki mani la. Delti, delti, delti o.

It is senseless not to be in your centre of power. It is senseless not to be in your power, your power that is given to you by the Source.

The Source feeds you. The Source looks after you. The Source expects you to know its role. Your nerves, your bodily functions, your organs are fed by the Source.

The Source is presenting you with choices: you can entirely depend on the Source, no food or otherwise required; you can entirely depend on your physical 3-D provisions, which results in a weak constitution and nerves; or, you can live in between, being more and more aware of the Source, of how it can help you, how it sustains you.

Be blessed by knowing that the Source is helping you, sustaining you. The more you trust your Source, the more you are blessed with a strong, healthy constitution and nerves. Once you know that you can entirely rely on your Source, you can be sure that less and less of you will rely on physical sustenance.

Capable of lifting you from the lowest to the highest, the Source of course does not interfere with your wants and your decisions. The Source is ever so mindful of your wishes. Your will is prevalent and is always respected by the Source. That is the law.

You are the one living this. If you tap into the Source and ask for more you will be given more. If you do not know about your Source, the Source does not stagnate. It subtly announces itself until you take notice. But still, it does not cajole you. It does not force you into doing anything. All are your decisions, all are your actions. And when you know and ask, expect wonderful things to happen to you.

The Source is ever mindful of where you are, how you understand your link to the Source and how it is always supporting you. The Source is waiting for you to awaken. The Source rejoices when that happens and remains ever so mindful, waiting for you to act, to ask for more.

So go ahead and ask your Source, your maker and creator. Ask him to stay with you throughout the day, throughout your life. Ask her to advise you, to support you, to help you, to be with you at all times. Listen for the subtle nudging, listen for the answers, and above all, trust. Trust that once you know and start asking, the Source will respond, will support you and guide you through your life in your dimension.

There is a hierarchy of things in the universe. Did you know that?

What do you mean?

What is it? It is a step down or step up, depending on which end you look at in the hierarchical organization of the elements of the universe. First is the Godhead, then comes the rest.

What is the rest?

The rest is the dimensional structure, which contain beings and consciousnesses who perform their responsibilities and acts of their own kind.

Hierarchy exists everywhere, as organization is preferred to chaos. Those who are higher in the hierarchy are in charge of those who are lower. We do not mean to say that all below are controlled. What we mean is that those in higher echelons do not only look after their own but are also in charge of some lower dimensional spheres to enable the living conditions there. The power is distributed and corresponds to the level of consciousness of the entities involved.

Hierarchy is most important when decisions are made. The power of higher wisdom and clarity is then wielded. Clarity and wisdom grow with the higher echelons of the hierarchy. The hierarchical structure is fed through the evolution of consciousness, meaning that you cannot buy into the hierarchical step above yours.

The hierarchy is mindful of the Source, as the Source is and always will be the leading source. It cannot be otherwise. The Source is the head, Godhead of all. Without the Source, there is nothing. Without the Source there is no life—no songs, no birds, no beings, nothing.

But hey, nothing is also of the Source. Void, the deepest void, is also of the Source. There is nothing without the Source and the Source is always. There is no other way. That is the law. The law is as this: the Source has been, is, and always will be. The Source is creation that is always happening. The Source is life that is always unfolding. The Source is nothingness that is flowing into beingness. The Source is a void that is getting ready to be. Nothingness into fulfillment, fulfillment into nothingness.

The cycle goes on and is never broken. The cycle is forever and is ever happening. The cycle is eternal. From void and nothingness, to life and fulfillment, diminishing back to void and nothingness. All is as it is. From sleep to awakening, from awakening to sleep. Such is the rhythm of your beingness.

The Source is and will be always your protector, your saviour. The Source is you. The Source is never separated from you. Whether you know it or not, the Source is always supporting you, is always with you. The Source is, and you are an extension of that Source.

And to realize that fully, understand this: the Source is waiting for your full awakening, for your full journey of coming back to your Source. The Source knows that you will, so be patient, be calm. Be sure that wherever you are, you are always at the place you need to be. The Source is with you and knows about you.

And that is all for now. You may go and take a break.

≪≫

Desi mu nati e. Eti pu? Eti mino a loa ti? Seti pul aoti duli ka si o mila. Mi la tu la oti pu neti mani sotiku. Ela ti elati muni la. Oti pu re mano ati me. Se tu akali mu omi ne seti la seti la omi nu le oti ke si pu omi no.

There is a wise saying: do not improve upon perfection. The words we dictated above are perfectly aligned to harmonize with your (the writer's) apprehensive nature. Soothing right to the bone. Best is to listen and not to think of the meaning. Do not think if it is typed right. Just let yourself soak up these sounds. Let yourself soak them up and be happy.

This is the beginning of your understanding. This is the beginning of your recognizing the calling of your soul, heard through the clamour of the material world. This is the voice of your soul that is coming to you.

It is a combination of trust and harmony that is so important. Bring harmony into your life. Bring harmony into your being. Bring harmony into your surroundings. Be pleased with what you have. Make it even prettier. Make it even more interesting. Be pleased with what you are doing. Be pleased with yourself.

Make yourself even more accessible. To your psyche. To your higher self. Be ready to reply when they ask questions. Be ready to listen when they talk to you. Be ready to be ready for them, as that is what they are there for. They are there for you, so make use of them. They are waiting to be contacted. They are waiting to hear from you.

"How do I do that?" you may ask. Well, keep on talking to them, calling them, trusting that they hear, trusting that they are here listening. Trusting. And one day you will hear with clarity. Perhaps a little voice at first. Perhaps a little suggestion at first. Then, more and more you will receive. More and more you will understand. More and more you will hear.

And then there will be no doubt about what you hear, what you do. You will talk to those who are your elders. Your higher self will be in conversation with you. Your I Am will converse with you.

Be ready for that occasion. It will be a sweet and happy event in your life to encounter those who are you, who have been waiting for you to discover your roots, to talk to them, to call them, to sing with them.

Helena, do you remember singing the Language of Light syllables when you were writing yesterday?

I do.

That's what it was. You sang as you wrote. You sang with them and you were so happy. You felt so calm. You were not in a hurry. You were not worried. You were singing and feeling the warmth of love coming to you. Yes, they beamed their love to you throughout your singing and that is why you were so happy and joyful.

That is how it works. Once you connect, your happiness is always with you. Once you connect, you will always find joy. Once you connect, you will always be ready to help those around you, as you know that you are helped as well.

As you know that state, you will help others acquire that state. As you know that happiness, you will help others find their happiness. Just you being with them, just your example will soothe them, will change them.

So be with your joy. Be with your highest purpose, knowing that when you connect that will be the end of your journey. When you connect and stay connected, you will know that your journey is at the end. You will no longer look for solutions. You will never again be unhappy. You will search no more. You will never be unfulfilled again.

That is a promise we can make, as we know ourselves. We still remember how we felt when we connected. That enormous joy, that joy of all joys. The world certainly changes. The world looks different. The world does not weigh on you anymore. The world becomes more transparent, not frightening. Fear no more. Do not be unhappy anymore. That is what will transpire when you meet those who have been waiting for you with loyalty and respect.

Es ti la ma ni moa. Seti la. Seti la mtit ona. Seti la seti la se it mu nomia ti. Seti la eti manu ti. Eti manu ti. Eti manu ti.

Sing the song of glory. Sing the song of glory to the angels waiting on you, to the people around you, to yourself. And with that, your I Am is sending you a message: "Persevere. Always persevere. You are on the right path. Never leave the path you have undertaken and you will succeed." Your I Am has spoken.

And that is all for today. Namaste and sayonara. We love you and we cherish you. Amen.

> Good night. I love you and thank you for all the messages.

Seti la, seti la.

Du no bi tu ale ki? Seti la seti la?

It is said that the God of all is watching and waiting.

Call your God, call her. Be with her. Tell her that you are expecting her love to shower you. Tell her that the love you want from her is all you need. There is no more than God's love directed to you.

God's love is all you need to wish for. God's love is all that you ever cared to have, as when you have God's love, you have everything. God's love is all giving. All soothing. All caressing. All encompassing.

All is included in God's love. God's love is available for taking. God's love is and always will be available. You receive God's love by asking for it. When you ask, it is given to you. When you do not ask, it is always there, however it is not directly applied to you by you. By asking for it, you receive it, as God cannot send it to you unless you ask. Your free will always prevails.

God, if asked to help you, will send all helpers to you. That is the way it is.

You can be sure that if you ask for help, you will receive it. If you ask for misery, you will receive it. If you ask for love, you will receive it. That is how it is.

Your love for God is returned tenfold. Your love for yourself is returned tenfold. You will be happy to hear that your love toward yourself will become God's love toward yourself. God is always ready to send you love if you love one of his children. If you love yourself, you, as God's child, will be rewarded. Your reward will be tenfold.

Deli mali oku. Seti la, seti la. Ati moni ku? Seti la seti la? Deli meni ati ko lu seti la seti la.

This is a message for all who believe that God is capable of great love toward them. Receive his love.

Receive his blessing. Receive, receive, receive. And be happy. Be happy.

Sile vu mi nu lo. Si le opulo. Sile vu sile vu sile vu. Domi noma ai oe. Sila meri aku te. Delti a ma na si mo. Tela ste munilo. Tela ste. Tela ste. Tela ste. Seti la. Manu ati prenula seti la. Seti la seti la.

During the privileged years of growing up and learning, many invite their God and Goddess to help with their growth. During the years of growth, always invite your God and Goddess. During the years of famine always invite your God and Goddess. Always be with your God and Goddess. Always.

That is today's message. Always be with your God and Goddess, does not matter what or where. Always call on your God and Goddess, does not matter how and how many times. Always speak to them, always call them. Always.

Vita meni ati lo. Seti la seti la. Ati mone deti ko. Seti la seti la. Seti ome nomi l kuli. Seti la seti la. Amoni kelimani toli oki monila. Seti la seti la seti la.

During times of disturbance, during the years of quiet, during the years of peace or wars, always call on your God and Goddess. Call them. Speak to them. At all times speak to them and call on them.

Deti la deti la ami no le koti. Deti la deti la moni le soti. Dila meno ait ke. Seti la seti. Moni mino seti la seti. Amoni seti la amono seti la. Deli kati omino peri seti oki tuli seti la.

And that is all. *Si li omin namisto.*

Amen and namaste. We love you and God loves you always.

∞

Eti la? Emi nu ope. Dari o me ni po si tu da ri ote la. De ri ma nome kom suti. Seti la mu no opi. Seti lu ma ne.

Call your God and Goddess. Bring them into your lives, as it is written that they do not come without you calling them. As it is written that they know you not until you know them. Do you know them? Call them and be with them. Call them and be entrenched in their love and generosity. Unconditional love and limitless abundance is yours. Unconditional love is yours to bask in.

Seti la seti la. Emu no mi po. Seti la seti la. Emi nu ope.

This is your awakening. This is your fearless awakening into the full realization of your God-given gifts. You can be anything you desire; singer, writer, painter. All of you have a seed of genius in you. Anything you can do is yours from God to cherish.

Seti la seti la. Menu ame no ti la. Seti la. Seti la.

Protected is a humble person who trusts in God. Protected is the one who is connected with God in his thoughts. Protected is the one. All he needs is to be with his God and Goddess. *Seti la seti la seti la.* Protected you are unless you feel fear of inadequacy, fear of being lost, fear of this and that.

Any fear is grounded in separation. Know your value comes from understanding your precious connection. *Seti la seti la seti la.* This connection is priceless. Cherish and grow this connection. Beyond your roving 3-D eyes, beyond your hearing 3-D ears, beyond your 3-D senses, there is life that goes on. There is continued life. There is that which you cannot yet see or hear, but some day you will be able to do so.

Seti la seti la.

This is a call that you need to listen to. It is the music of angels that you need to listen for. It is a spiritual feeling of piety that overcomes you once in a while. All these are the signs of your connection that has been and is, but is lost as your eyes and ears do not see nor hear. Know that it is still there. Know that it always will be there. The lost connection is there. You need to come to its last thread and unravel it, pull yourself up by it, closer and closer to your maker and creator.

Seti la seti la. Emi no me tu li pa si. Ani manu arote. Meni la seti koti amu. Nemi la oti la. Seti la seti la. Si si mi nu eti koti. Seti la omi no peru k mani opne lu. Seti la seti la seti la. Ok mu n per k ome no pi la tu. Seti la seti la seti la. Emu nao me re ti ku la seti la. Seti la seti la. Ku ru mu a no i? Ku ra ti pole si? Aki to me ni? Seti la seti la seti la. Ek te mu na oke? Seti la.

There is comfort in these syllables. There is comfort in the Language of Light. There is comfort in knowing that the strings of light bring you messages, connect you with your origins.

Seti la seti la is a call you came to unravel. *Seti la. Eti me nu opi la. Meni tu oke pu si te lu ku. Seti la seti la seti la. Menu ami no? Menu ami no? Seti la seti la. Menu ome nu li po. Seti la seti la seti la. Menu ome no. Menu le ki. Menu ole seti la. Bu li mani pore si keti alo. Seti la seti la seti la. Menu alo meni po. Seti la seti la seti la. Menu alo alo menu si lu okin dor. Seti la seti la seti la. Poli mu nami no es tila. O ke la po ti tul li ko te o ko mena minu seti la. A ko menu la. Peti lupi oke. Seti la. Veti o ka muni beti deri a ko me. No mi tu la oti me. Seti la seti la seti la. O ke meno moni o ka li pula ti. Deri tuli o ke mino seti la seti la seti la. A ko menu opi nola seti la seti la seti la. O ke meno o ke meno o ke meno. Seti la.*

Kuli meno ami no. Seti la pole a ko me. Seti la seti la. Best of all.

Helena, during this writing your healing progresses. As the syllables are uttered, your soul sends messages to you. Deep down in your body these are registered. The registration of these is an experience that is known to you from previous sessions. This time confusion reigns, as the words are many. Do not be impatient. You need to heal yourself. We work on all aspects of your being and this part is important. Do not shun from being in flow. Write what comes to you and cheerfully transcribe it. Type our dear, type.

Si kula mene, ati polu seti la. Aku mene duti ole piti mu ni ame la. Seti la seti la seti la.

This transmission is done. We would like you to come again today. No time is given.

> Thank you. Thank you for all your work. If I was impatient, I am not anymore. Amen.

Desi lu? Seti la seti la. Call your God and be well. Call your God and be happy. Call your God now and you will be rewarded. *Seti la seti la seti la.* Your I Am is your advisor. Your I Am is your best friend. *Seti la la seti la seti la. Seti la mi no me ti. Aki nomi seti la. Ake nomi ale mona seti la seti la. Ako ti meno mi ola tu li. Seti la. Ako me no mie. Seti la. Anomi akote reti meni anome. Ala tuli pote la. Seti la moni ako name. Reti aki sa ti le mi nome amona tolie ruti ako me neti seli no.*

Be with your God at all times. Be aware of him, be aware of his presence. Your God is within you, is caressing you, is upholding you. He is you and is controlling you not, but is sending his best love. You can take it or not. You can bask in it or not. Your will is free.

Your choices are your own. You can choose to act like a child of God or like a child of Beelzebub.

You are always connected to your Source, to your God, and it is up to you to utilize your connection. Be aware of this. Pray to him. Ask her to be in your decision making. Ask her to help you decide. Ask him to come and advise you. Ask her at all times and be ready to listen, as that is what you need to do.

Listen to your inner voice. Listen to your inner urges. Listen to your inner life. Within is where you need to listen, and then your within will be visible without, will live in your 3-D world and will guide you.

Your inner voice is your guidance. Your inner life is that which is connected to your God and Goddess. So listen to it. Be in tune with your inner voice and your feelings. Listen to them, do not dismiss them, do not discard them. Listen and act on them, and riches will be brought to you. Riches, unimaginable, beautiful riches.

Your connectedness with your Source will bring you all you dreamed possible and more. It will bring you peace. It will bring you calm. Peace and calm will then enable you to hear your inner voice even better. This will bring the understanding, the knowing, the wisdom. All the wisdom of the universe will be at your fingertips.

You link to your Source via the heart. Observe your feelings. Those are your guiding posts. Consult your heart. Consult your feelings. Your heart knows and your feelings tell you. Does it feel good? Does it feel strange?

If you ask your heart to tell you how it feels, it will help you to live the way you were meant to live. In awe of all creation. In awe of life itself. In pleasure and happiness. In awe of your own ability to connect and understand.

You create your destiny, so you and only you can take your destiny into your hands and live as you were intended to live. Without fear. Without hate. Without malnutrition and poverty. Live with joy in the connectedness and knowingness that your maker and creator is always standing by you.

We wish you all the best in this. Achieve what you desire. Be in tune. Be connected. Be aware. Come on, come on, we urge you to live your potential.

In conclusion of this transmission, we would like to call upon all the saints and ascended masters, all angels and archangels, your I Am, to pray for the awakening of the inhabitants of Earth. Pray for their awakening to their powerfulness, to their creative powers, to heartfelt ways of living.

We pray and ask God to support this process that will bring the inhabitants of Earth to their centre of power and enlightenment to masses of people. It will lift them from poverty of thought and physical means. It will lift them toward a glorious, all knowing future.

And that is all for today. Please come back tomorrow and we will continue. We love you and we cherish you. Be well and stay as beautiful as you are. Amen.

Chapter Ten

We Are Speaking to You from the Dimension of Light

We are speaking to you from the Dimension of Light. We are speaking to you from a dimension where our concern is to help those who are living on Earth to understand fully who they are, to understand their origins. Once the awareness is there and the veil of forgetfulness is lifted, we help and facilitate your return until you need to return no more. We can be facilitators only to those who grasp this concept. We do not facilitate those who cannot at this point in their lives believe that this reality is their own reality.

We do not act against anybody's will. That is the law. Your will is foremost and we only help if we are asked. Otherwise, we are patient and wait for the opening to become available. We go and help those who have asked us to help them. Such is the order of the universe. Your will is foremost.

Once we have your attention and once you are ready to approve of what we say, once you trust it, we can and will always help.

We need to stress that this help is many-fold. It is in the form of messages, promptings, feelings, exalted, blissful moments that show the way. But beware, you are the way-showers, you are your own path seekers. All is your impetus, we are only facilitators. We will not drag anybody screaming and kicking against their will. We will not push, prod nor pull. That is not the law. The law is for us to gently guide you to take a step or an action. Is that clear?

If you have promptings that are incomprehensible to you, trust that if you stay with them, you will come to a point where a revelation will come to you. The next point comes after a similar process, and then again. You always are where you need to be, but because of your current abilities, you may not understand. Your promptings may make you question or feel uneasy. You may not understand them or why you are asking such questions.

And that is fine. That is how the knowledge will be revealed to you. Stay with your intuition. If your intuition is hinting, is prompting, there is something you need to pay attention to. Stay within and ask: "Why am I asking these questions? What is it I am asking for?" Ask your God, your maker, to help you find the source of your uneasiness, your curiosity. If you keep asking and continue with your probing, your efforts will always be recognized and help will be sent to you. It may be a clear message, a book, or a person that comes into your life and leads you toward a new event or information that will change the course of your life.

You call such events coincidences. Well, there are none. Nothing is a coincidence. All events in your life have a reason and a deeper meaning that you come to trust. If not right away, more of these "coincidences" occur and finally you will recognize that which is sent to you.

We think Helena that this is enough for now. We need you fresh and not tired. We need you to feel that we co-operate with you, not that we dictate. We love you, we love you so much. Get well and stay well. Okay? Say, "I am well, I am strong and healthy. I am well and will always be." Resonate with love and all that is ailing you will pass. Resonate with love and all will pass.

And that is all. Go and take a break. We are happy that you showed up. Namaste and sayonara.

The millennium passing of this century is a time of changes toward better alignment of the planet Earth with those planets that are already in the 5th dimension. We would like to recommend to those who are open, that you, as inhabitants of the Earth, align yourselves with this event.

This is the theme of this century – alignment with the Earth coming to the 5th dimension. Alignment with those who are progressing into the 5th dimension. Align yourself with the prevalent trend of your universe. Align yourself, as that is where you belong. You are the citizens of this universe. Do not stay behind and you will progress to bigger spirited activities.

This message was brought to you by the Peacekeepers, by the Universal Peacekeepers and Peace Setters.

Now we are calling The Federation Society to continue.

The trend of alignment with the 5th dimension is the theme of the times. We need to caution you—if you are not ready, do not try. There will be, and there already have been, many opportunities. This is not a one-time chance to move on. This is one of many occasions, and you will continue your progression when you are ready, not just the circumstances around you. With this, we would like to call upon Archangel Michael.

Michael, is there any information you would like to add?

"Yes. This is a message from the realm of angels and archangels. Angelic beings are in droves surrounding your planet Earth. We all are ready to facilitate the birth of your new world. We all are singing with joy, as after many upheavals we see peace, calm, and understanding coming to you. We are ready to help to transform, transpose, and transfigure those who are prepared to leave the 3-D Earth, those who are prepared to continue their lives on Earth helping others, or those in other dimensions. Angels are visiting your planet often at this time. The number of angels and visitations are rising. We need to accomplish the helping of many, as the times are moving along quickly. We need to move on with you, as by facilitating your new beginnings, we are facilitating our new beginnings. All is connected. All is one."

"The energies are moving from one dimension to another through portals and vortexes that are closed and opened according to the veils and energies possessed by those who are coming through these portals. We cannot describe enough the joy and excitement in our spheres, as this is an event we have been expecting for a long time. This event is of the highest order and is supported by the Source and all gods and goddesses of the Universes. We are privileged to be of service to you. We are privileged to participate and play an important role in these times of unrest and upheavals, followed by peace and understanding. Hang in there. You are in for the ride of your lives. This century will not be forgotten. It will be embedded deeply into the psyche of humanity. Historians will be in awe for centuries to come and the progress will be of such a level that humanity could never have imagined these types of gains–love, understanding, openness. The knowledge of your origins will be multiplied many times. We are done." Michael.

Thank you Michael.

I Am of all nations is speaking, "I am speaking to all. Be within and examine your motives. Be within and do not compare yourself with others. It is you who matters to you, not others. It is you, only you, who can make a difference, not others. If you consider others, you forget your own role. If you all rule through your heart, others will rule through their hearts, as that is how it works. So others do not matter. It is you who matters. More and more realize this truth, and more and more be with those who are ruling through their heart. This is I Am of all nations. Namaste. Amen."

Thank you all for coming. We would like to now talk about Jesus Christ. Jesus Christ is an advanced, accomplished soul that resides in the 14th dimension right now. This soul lived upon Earth approximately 2000 years ago. This entity overcame the 3-D constraints of his life and accomplished that which you are pursuing right now en masse. He ascended to his creator. He ascended to show humanity, who as such did not understand what it meant at the time. It did not matter that much to them that Jesus was resurrected. His resurrection was to show that overcoming the body is within your power.

He ascended to show humanity that overcoming the physical senses is something that you all can do. That matter is not dominant, that it is the spirit that guides you. That the spirit is the most prevailing aspect of your being.

That is all for today. We would like to thank all for coming. Namaste and sayonara. We love you and we cherish you. Amen.

Helena, we have an energetic beam that we can send you. Do you accept?

Yes, I accept.

Fine. It is coming now. Sit straight and receive.

Right. Received. Thank you.

Good. Let us begin.

We would like to present today a story, a story of the beginnings and the decay of an empire called "A Saintly Reign of Angels". This story has a multitude of similarities with what is happening to humanity today.

This reign of angels was known to be of angels dedicated to their own kind. With great care, they prepared their members to achieve greatness. They achieved their prominence in the psychic sciences and were on the verge of becoming a race ready to move on. A few, who saw the psychic sciences as a way of deluding others and enriching themselves, hampered this process. This took hold and the race did not advance, as that was no longer possible. They were catapulted into another reality and were ready to achieve great things again; however, an unfortunate sequence of events pulled them down once more into an abyss of forgetting their divinity. This scenario has repeated itself many times. We are not sure if this scenario will repeat itself yet again, or whether they will realize their divine plan and potential.

This race was catapulted once again and ended up ... guess where? At your place. You, as many of you are descended angels, are grasping with your 3-D reality and that is where we are at now—talking to you, the descended angels. Your angelic and divine origins have been forgotten. Your angelic and divine origins are not upheld by your acts and approach. You must shed your 3-D roots, as you are without a doubt rooted here. You must become a race of angels that catapult themselves into disarray no more, that catapult themselves into an orbit of higher wisdom and realization of their higher origins.

We would like you to ponder this. Spread this knowledge. Let others know. Be ready to escalate your own godliness. Be ready to escalate your own understanding of your origins. We are ready and stationed to help you at all times.

That is all for today. Namaste.

Thank you. Namaste.

❧ ❧

Da ti mo ne oki. Si tu ome noti. Roti tu la ako ty mu. Situ la me oni du. Delti ami nome ti. Si tu o ne meno ti. Dul ti o me noti mi sesti mone dela ti. Kula ti kule mi aoki mon no so al ti. Dul it dul ti mone li. M ne.

Your I Am is calling and is talking to you. Your I Am is thinking of you. Your I Am is with you at all times.

> *I am calling you my I Am. I want to be with you my I Am. I am that I Am.*

No me si la ti. Nomi sila nomi sila. Eti tu mi la. So ti la sutil. Meni omi kote preti. Tula imo omi nomi ma.

There is a wealth of information in these words. There is a wealth of information in the entire universe. There is a wealth of information and the chosen will receive it. Who will choose them? Themselves. You choose that which is your vibrational counterpart. You choose that which vibrates the way you do. You choose the vibrational frequency that is close to you. Your vibrations undulate through the universe. Your vibrations are heard and seen and are always undulating, coming and leaving.

We all are a pool of vibrational fields. We all are vibrations at different frequencies. If the frequency is slow and dull, matter is more visible. If the frequency is high and clear, matter is not visible. Matter, as in physical matter, is a frequency slowed down to a dull, slow level where all slows down and congeals. Still, there is movement in your perception, in your body, in your cells, that links you to your maker and caretaker, your God and Goddess.

We want to be clear on this: the frequency fields, non-polluted, direct from the God Source energy, mix with other pure, non-polluted energy. This mixing happens when the frequencies match. Matches are found and replenished throughout the universe. The universe finds the match that is yours and delivers an exact or similar match. When this occurs, you can become a transmitter for the messages that are suitable to be sent to the point at which you are.

Sending messages is not difficult; it is the receiving part that may be more complicated. The messages "match" the recipient. They are then translated into "foreign content" which matches the receiver's ability to understand, and then retranslated to the living language of the person. We can go into more detail, but that is not required at this time.

When you meditate, your frequency rate increases. Your body clarifies itself and your receptors become able to receive the content of a much higher spiritual power. This is why we urge you to meditate, to be disciplined about it. All the conscious striving raises your frequency. All lazing around dulls your frequency.

There are other elements that can influence the transmission. There are also other ways to receive, particularly with people who are already highly evolved in the spiritual aspect. However, we shall not delve further into this subject at this time.

These pointers were meant for the writer. Of course, they are applicable to many other people.

> *Above, you used the term non-polluted energy.*
> *Please explain.*

The term "non-polluted" energy refers to energies emanating directly from the Source. They are emitted constantly from the Source to bring new, refreshed energies into circulation. They are vibrationally intact, as they have not compromised themselves by choosing frequencies that are not their match. Therefore, the term "polluted" energy would refer to energies that have combined with frequencies that are not the same as their own.

How do energies mix?

Non-polluted energies coming from the Source are on the lookout for other non-polluted fields of energy. They are on the lookout for their equal counterparts, energies of the same frequencies, to combine and enlarge their field to increase their influence. When a match is found, the energies copulate, so to speak, and create fields that are new.

What happens then?

The evenly spaced frequencies are distributed to appropriate locations, such as your planet, to live and grow together. They live and multiply in their respective areas where they proliferate. They combine to experience oneness. Oneness is the experience that all want to know, as it is not that easy to be alone.

Please explain the term polluted energy.

It is such that the energies interlace, trying to get the match as close as possible together but this does not always happen. It is not an exception, but matches that are exact are not easy to get.

It is an approximation the energies are looking for. When that happens, the energies are happy to proliferate and learn from the process. When energies combine and their frequencies are not same, they become what we term "polluted". However, this term does not indicate that they are unclean.

How do the energies combine?

When they find a match, they copulate—energy heats up and predisposes itself to either enter or accept the other energies. Then of course the inevitable happens– copulation, success—and a new combined energy is born.

When does it happen?

Whenever possible. This happens freely and frequently.

And why does this happen?

Because of curiosity, wanting new experiences, wanting companionship, wanting a new baby so to speak, change. All of those and more.

That is all for now. We love you and we cherish you. Amen.

Direct messaging is possible through acquiring telepathic skills. This is soon to come to some people of this Earth. In fact, a few have already acquired these skills. This is to better facilitate communication. To be able to develop this quality, the body needs to be healthy and supported by proper food and pure water. When we say soon, from your perspective that means within a century you will see more people acquire such skills.

Those people who already use telepathy are few and far between. They are often people who live in monasteries and retreats, where their lives are devoted to their spiritual selves.

You may believe that telepathy is a part of science fiction that has never happened or never will be. Well, change your attitudes. Change your beliefs. You have the power to change, remember? With a different set of beliefs you will start listening to your feelings and finding that sometimes you know what people are thinking, what they are going to say. This is not yet telepathy. Rather, it is a precursor to the beginning of your understanding of how you work.

Allow yourself to doubt all your preconceived ideas about the world. Allow yourself to be open and you will find many options and events available to you that at first you thought not possible. When you meditate, allow yourself to drift into a place of no time, no space, and eventually you will inhabit different planes via your consciousness.

All this, telepathy and direct messaging, will come to be within the next century. This is not to say that all will have these capacities, however, these qualities will be visible and more prevalent in the century to come.

Helena, we would like you to take a break now.

We appreciate your coming back so soon. There is a change in our plan. This transmission will be shorter than what we had at first intended.

We were talking about telepathy to come. There are other changes that will also be visible. Apart from telepathy, your understanding of your origins will be better.

You will not know exactly, but you will comprehend that beyond this planet of yours is a dimension that is not entirely foreign to you, and that you have visited it many, many times. Some of you will know more than you would like. As this dimension is expanding its realm to encompass other dimensions like yours, you will hear about it from many sources and will in time be able to drift into it, through various means of your skills or other means.

You said, "There are other changes that will also be visible". What does that mean?

Well, let us say some of you will come into an awareness about the existence of other dimensions while living on Earth. Some of you will visit them after you leave this planet.

That is all for now. Namaste and sayonara.

Namaste, and thank you.

Deri suti ma? Oti le? Seti la seti la. Meti oki no ri tu. Esti mueno li ta. Kuti ake so ti la. Ami no seti la. Omi nome oki tu-li. Reti oniko suli ome no. Seti la seti la seti la. Oki nova seti la oki nova seti la. Beli moki tuli oka seti la seti la seti la. Oki nomi na. Meni tu la oki no. Seti la seti la seti la. Omoni seti la. Omoni seti la. Omoni.

We are delighted to be working with you Helena. We are delighted to be a part of your progress. We marvel at your production. It is a production of your soul, of your I Am transferring to you, and you back. You served in this capacity for many ages and that is what your specialty is—to listen and to pass on. Listen well and pass it on to your contemporaries.

We are pleased to be able to explain this process. There are many connections of your doing. You are not only using those that have been established before, but are constantly creating new ones as well. You are listening through your ethereal crystal embedded in your skull, particularly in your 3rd eye. Crystals are embedded in other parts of your body as well. They intercept and ponder the meaning of the messages, then take appropriate action to transmit them to the appropriate places. The crystals do not make these decisions alone. Your higher self and yourself are all at work. Your higher self, for instance, facilitates this transmission.

This transmission is uncomplicated, as many prepared the way to a clear transmission in goodwill of receiving information that concerns humanity. Many participate in this endeavour: your higher self, your I Am, the angels and those beings of the light whose purpose is to watch over humanity. We will not count or describe them one by one, but remember, these beings are your link to the dimension of the light. They have always worked on humanity's behalf.

Many are receiving messages. Many are talking to their guides and angels. Many are listening and recording. There are interplanetary communications going on. Many are in contact with extraterrestrial beings. We all are getting connected. We all are seeking further knowledge. We all are looking for answers. Everywhere, we all are seeking and progressing toward the purest, most beautiful light of God.

We are working with many. Thus, we are experiencing the shifting moods and experiences of many. This also helps us in shifting and experiencing the connections that are beyond our worlds.

You need to see these connections, these links. They have spread and grown. They have been evident for millennia and dimensions are spanning in between. These connections are still working and are visible. They are cultured and not so. They are scientific and not so. They are of all flavours and predicaments, joys, happiness and unhappiness. They still exist and have been preserved for many other transmissions to come.

That is all for now. We like you to come back at least once more today. Sayonara and namaste. Amen.

Beti mu no. Ati pu. Le ti ome. Nati mu.

Humanity is not sure of their origins. Some think they are descendents of apes. Humanity neglected their spiritual part and forgot their spiritual self. This message aims to open that communication again, as communication with the spirit is essential. Communication with the spirit is essential to awaken the majority of humanity.

This project is essential. It is important to life on this planet. It is life-threatening not to be connected to your Source. It is life-giving to realize that your Mother-Father God within yourself is expecting you to wake up and call. Call them, call them. Ask them to help. Call them to come and help. Ask them to stay with you. Ask them to be with you at your every step throughout your life.

Communicate your wants. Communicate your dreams. Communicate whatever pleases you. Tell them all. Ask for forgiveness. Ask for joy. Ask for anything you need to ask. And keep on asking. Do not forget the next day. Keep at it until the communication is open and becomes so clear that there is no doubt that you are talking to your God within.

This message is so important. Do not belittle this message or the messenger. Do not belittle the importance of open communication with your maker. Ask her to be with you, to help you, to guide you, to assist you. If you ask her for assistance, you are assisting yourself. If you ask her for help, you are helping you. By helping yourself, you will help others. By assisting yourself, you will assist others. This is the law. What is done to you is done to all. That what you do to yourself, you do to others. This law needs to be upheld. Do not do anything to you that you do not want done to others. Such is the law.

Misli ta mi ne ti mu? Ati pela ki to? Der ta, de tia. Mi la mi no aom ta. Seti la. Seti la. Seti la.

Your I Am is speaking now. Your I Am is here. Your own progress is important, as it is a mirror of the progress that is happening to others. This mirror held to your face will show you that communicating with your God and Goddess is the way. Why is it essential that you communicate? It is essential that you open the link of communication and that you become so close that you know your creator guides you at all times, leads you to where you will benefit the most, to your full understanding of your dual nature – spiritual and physical.

Humanity does not understand the dual nature of theirs. It is not understood and it is shunned. The link needs to be re-established and kept open.

Link yourself with your God. Through your God, you are linked to all. Through your God, you breathe and live as one. Through your God, you are all as one entity. Understand that and be happy that you have found the way to come back to your God. Just trust and believe. Trust and believe. Talk to your God. Trust that she hears. Trust that she listens. Trust that she answers. Trust, trust, trust.

Trust your spiritual nature. Uphold your spiritual nature. Be in your heart and not in your mind. Be in your heart.

Namaste and sayonara. Be well. We love you and we cherish you. Be back tomorrow morning. Amen.

Namaste. Amen.

Chapter Eleven

In Closing

Eclectic or not, these pages are packed with advice. We only prescribe remedies that you can use. If we were to prescribe remedies that are beyond the scope of your understanding, we would not be doing you any good.

We would like to thank all who have participated in this project. There is more to this endeavour than meets the eye. Aside from the scribe and receiver, there are other beings involved. It is like a relay—the information is received at one station and is sent on to another station, and so on. This is cooperation of cosmic proportions, you may say.

This is a vital project for all concerned to move, to discard all that is not viable and sustainable anymore. Move on to your true Self. Move on to Your Self that is supportive of you. You are the object of its support. You can be coddled by your Source if you let the energies come to you and support you. Ask for them to be with you. Ask for them to support you. Allow them to come and do their work. Let them come to you and trust that you are being looked after, as you always are and have been.

This message would not be complete without the interjection of the following:

Many have access to this information. Many are receiving similar messages. Many are playing hard to get, as they do not trust themselves. This occasion is one of those when the scribe knows that the source is pure. Trust has been established.

Trust is needed for all this to work, to come to those who need it, to receive the knowledge they have been looking for.

We are thrilled to be a part of this project. We are thrilled to be able to participate. So is Helena, although she still harbours some confusion about the result. Do not dwell on these thoughts Helena. Be open to your maker's messages and information. Be open and know that you are protected.

Any time before you sit down to receive messages, always ask for the purest light and unconditional love to come to you. Always stipulate that no others, no other energies need come. You are the type of receiver who is an open venue to many transmissions. Thus, the assurance that only the highest possible, purest light and love come through is vital to the success of this and future projects.

We are pleased that all is continuing and is being so received with ease. Via the heart, all is done with peace and calm. Via the mind, confusion and debates reign. With the heart, all is clear and the information received can be classified without too much effort. Don't you feel a surge of joy when you know something feels right? That is your heart talking to you. That is your heart rejoicing in the fact that you are a receiver and listener, and that you are connected to your Source.

The Source is open and is sending information at all times. All is available through your Source. Technical information, spiritual insights, all is available as The Source is the source. It is the source of all.

Nothing that is conceived and used on Earth is of purely human origin. All are signals and messages received and interpreted for the 3-D environment. All that is discovered is information already in existence. Therefore, you can say that nothing is new. Nothing is newly discovered.

When there is the "right time" for the information to come through, it will come. It is the right time and the right circumstances that allow the interception of "new" ideas. That is how Edison worked. That is how Tesla received his information and came out with new discoveries and patents. They were blessed by quieting their minds and intercepting the information from the pool of total consciousness.

Information is always received this way. The receptor is open to accepting the message coming through. The receptor knows that it is time to receive this material and make it available to others.

The receptor, Helena, is poised to be of service to us and human kind. This receptor has been groomed for many lifetimes and has already served in a similar capacity several times. This receptor is getting better and better and her direct knowledge of her ability will now enhance the quality of information coming through. We can only marvel at the speed of her receiving. We like the tempo and we like the flow. It is all natural and easy going. Such is the ease of the process that we do not mind an occasional break for 3-D activities. The flow of the material is not interrupted. We have been blessed to be working with someone like Helena. She is a fine individual and understands the importance of this project for this time you all live in.

So, with that we adjourn you all and be ready to continue later today. Namaste and sayonara. Thank you and talk to you soon. May you all live in the highest, purest light and love. Namaste again.

We are the messengers; we are those who are with enthusiasm seeking to disperse the knowledge to humanity. We are not seeking the role of saviours. We only want to contact humanity to make them aware of all aspects of their lives.

What you call death is not the annihilation of yourself. It is not the end. It is the beginning of another epoch of your lives. You cannot die. You simply change from being in your body to a free spirit. Your dead are as alive as you are, even more than you are. When you "die" you will rejoice in seeing those you thought you would never see again.

As always, it is your will and consciousness that prevail. If you believe that there is a heaven and hell, and if you believe you do not deserve to go to heaven, guess what happens? Of course, you end up in hell. A hell of your own making. As you imagine it, so hell is. You believe it, so it will be yours. Does that mean that hell exists? Of course not. As soon as you come to this realization, your own imaginary hell will go poof and you will be wherever you think you should be.

It all depends on you. You may ask, "And how does it depend on me?" As we said before, it is your mind, it is your consciousness.

And the story goes on. You are a story weaver, your own spell weaver, your own life story writer, a player, and that is how it is. You better understand that sooner than later, as that is what you are heading toward anyway. So, what's the delay? Or, shall we say, what's the rush? Some of you have been doing it for millennia.

The universe is full of beings of different forms, physical or other. These beings report to their maker once in a while like you do. However, their understanding is deeper and they do not fear the afterlife, or as you call it, death. Dying is not a process of annihilation. Dying is a process of rebirth to the place of your beginnings. It is the place of your yearnings. You yearn to come back. You yearn to inherit the Kingdom of God. You yearn to come and join those who went before you. You yearn to rediscover how it was before you were born to Earth. Those yearnings are known to us, as we are those who lived as humanity on the planet Earth and left many times to come back again and again, until we no longer needed to.

No one lives solely in the 3-D. There are other aspects of you. There are other lives you live. You may be surprised by this thought, but that does not change its validity. You live on many levels. You are multifaceted.

You can be many places at the same time, and you are. Do blink on and off to see where you are. If you are here with us, it is in a dream state. If you clean your home, your room, you are more in the 3-D aspect of your life. As Helena types, she is in between, as she is intercepting these messages. What we are saying is that there is more to you.

There is more to you than meets the eye. Your roving eyes cannot see the beauty of other places and dimensions.

Of course, your Earth is also beautiful. It is a wonder of wonders. It is a place of immense beauty. However, its pristine beauty is being scarred and polluted nowadays more than ever.

With sadness, we are noticing the yellow plumes of pollution about your big cities. With sadness, we are noticing the polluted murky rivers and streams. With sadness, we are noticing that you are not as healthy as you used to be. Many of you breathe heavily. Many of you walk heavily. Many of you are not even aware of your existence apart from working, eating and going to sleep. You merely exist and survive from one day to another.

Wake up! Please wake up! There is more to you than you can imagine. There is more to you. Find out about you. It is you who is calling you. Your higher self is calling you, is asking you to wake up, to come to your home, to come back to your origins. To be with the stellar performance of your soul. To be with the stellar performance of your I Am. Be ready to face the fact that the physical is not enough. It is not enough. There is more to you. You are a multifaceted being.

Be aware that there are many here who can help you. There are many here who are already helping you. Just get up and ask. Call us and we will come and serve you. By serving you, we are serving ourselves. By helping you, we are helping ourselves.

That is the law. What we do for others we do for ourselves. What we do to ourselves, we are doing to others. We are connected. We are one. We feel the same.

We are ready. Ask us, call us. We will reply. That is what we are waiting for. We need your cooperation. When we say call, we mean it. Call us. We want you to call us. We want you to ask many questions. We want you to persevere and always be ready to get help.

Trust your God and Goddess. Trust, and your trust will be rewarded. You will become leading experts on that which is your body and spirit. Become one that pursues one's own joy, abundance and happiness.

We are waiting for you to make up your mind. Call us. We are waiting.

Sayonara and be ready.

Apropos, we are happy to see you, Helena, getting better. Amen.

You live amidst upheavals and misunderstandings. You live in times when many die needlessly. You live in times when terror, war and killing reign. You believe in "an eye for an eye". You believe that you can only win by killing those who kill your own. This is breeding contempt and continuation of the killing spree. This is not where humanity can dwell.

Humanity needs to move beyond its own deranged beliefs. Humanity needs to come together and know that you all are one.

Don't you understand that you live on your Earth, the planet of beauty? You are one, you are taken for a ride on your planet, you have nowhere else to go. Why this senseless hatred of different races? Why these senseless killings? Why this horrible endless warring and hatred spilling from one country to another. Why? Have you sunk so low that you have no understanding of your origins? Are you in such a state of disrespect for your psyche and soul that you only get satisfaction from gore and carnage?

Look at your entertainment. What brings big money? Is it love and peace? No. It is fear, horror, carnage, blood, killing, maiming, ghosts and monsters. Is that how low you have sunk? So it seems.

But hope is everlasting. Trust in your origins is strong. Just a few who trust can ignite the sacred flame in your hearts. Then that flame will grow stronger and stronger, and will reintroduce peace, understanding, and love to all mankind. We see it happening. Those who are in the advanced stages of their lives will not be able to see any big changes toward the peaceful nature of man. But those who are very young will live in a different world, and they know that it will come. That is why they are here now at their young tender age. They have a role to play.

They have the role of rebuilding this planet to the point where all nations work together as one, where all sources of riches in your soil, land and water belong to all. No nation, no country will make claims on "their" natural resources.

There will be an understanding that those resources belong to all, but first of all, to Mother Earth. She will decide how they will be distributed. She will comply with her heart and help those who are the most in need. She is the maker and distributor of all natural resources and there is no better way than to rely on her.

Your Mother Earth knows. Be guided by her and be guided by the spirit that dwells in you. Be guided. Be guided by your heart, and all will be as it was intended to be. Those who facilitate changes, those who understand the concept of their origins and work through their heart, will move on to other dimensions to work on even more exciting projects. Their own evolution will take a qualitative leap that will propel them toward their maker, closer and closer.

With the coming Earth changes, we would again like to stress that the change in humanity needs to match the Earth changes. Is the Earth cleansing? So need you. Is the Earth taking steps to renew herself? So need you. Is the Earth getting rid of that which does not work? You need to do that as well. Is the Earth coming to the conclusion that certain aspects of it need to go? So is humanity.

The Earth needs to cleanse, and it will, as that is necessary for any body. It is not going to blow itself up as some are trying to predict. Once it settles down, it will be renewed and ready for a higher dimensional experience.

Some of you will decide to leave. All will leave who know they need to leave. Nobody leaves without knowing this at the level of his or her higher self. It is a collaboration of all your aspects, weighing your options, weighing your progress, weighing your understanding of your accomplishments, weighing your readiness. You all need to ask: "Am I ready to stay here, or do I need to leave?"

During the cleansing of Mother Earth many will die, but only those who know that they need to or because they prefer to leave. Without your agreeing and understanding you cannot be taken away. Your free will expands through all aspects of you—you on Earth and those aspects of you that are in the ethereal and spiritual realms.

Project Earth, as we call it, is not on time as you understand it, but is on time, as we understand it here. It is quality changes that measure our time.

We can see that the needle is nearing that time when quality changes will come into place, and many changes will appear thereafter in your dimension. You all will be notified either by your own self, your intuition, or others that are more in tune with their inner feelings and knowing.

That is all for now. With that we adjourn you all, and be ready to continue later today. Namaste and sayonara. Thank you and talk to you soon. This was The Federation for Peace. May you all live in the highest, purest light and love. Namaste again.

Dire mi tu la. Esi tu? Bila mi no epi naki. Situ le mo ni. Seti la seti la seti la.

Events are unfolding. Thunder is coming and a nice hue of red is approaching. What is it? Is it a war on the horizon? Is it a dewy sunrise? You decide, as you all are makers of your destiny.

Do not be driven by greed. Do not be driven by comforts of life that do not comfort you, but rather strangle you. Do not be ready to abdicate all that is honourable.

Be ready to stand up for the biodiversity of the planet. For the blessing of all life. Be ready to stand up for life that was created naturally.

Si su meni opi na, ati ko le mi. Seti la. Seti la seti la.

During the 2nd World War, a trend was set. The reverse is about to happen.

Seti la seti la seti la. Amino meti kulu a. Seti la seti la seti la. Amino kuli ato pu. Seti la seti la seti la. Amino seti tuli oma. Seti la seti la seti la seti la. Amino seti la. Me k.

War is about fighting against the enemy, so they say. But where is the enemy? There is only you, and you are fighting yourself. Your inability to see this with clarity is keeping you from realizing that the brotherhood and sisterhood of people is a way of ascertaining your love rather than your hatred for one another. It is about expressing your kindness rather than conflict toward your fellow being.

During these last years of unrest, all will become clear. All is as it needs to be, as darkness cannot be without light, and light cannot be without darkness. That is the way to perceive it.

Light spills into darkness, but darkness does not spill into light. See for yourself. Open the door to a dark room and see if the darkness spills out. It does not. The light from where you are spills into the darkness. That is the law, and we beg you to uphold the natural law. We beg you to uphold all that is natural, that which is of the creator of all.

Seti la seti la meti oku na. Seti la seti la meti seti mu la me tu ki. Ki shu meni ako ti. Seti la.

There is a lot of truth in these words. There is an element of truth in everything. If you hear something, do not discard it completely. Nothing is without some truth. Certain truths are more obscure than others. Certain truths are harder to find than others, but know that your truth does not always have to match other people's truths. Of course, there are always prevalent truths that never, ever change, such as kindness and unconditional love.

Seti mi na ku? Seti la. Esti dole meno ti? Seti la. Seti la omi no pula ti. Seti la seti la.

During times of crisis, there are truths and then there are truths. All have their own truth to help them keep their own, sometimes misguided, dignity. All have their own truth, but the real truth is the universal law of truth.

Universal law of truth? What is that?

It is "the" truth. It is the truth that is not menacing, that is soft and hard at the same time. It is not a construed truth. It is not a truth that is thought up.

It is the truth that is universal, the truth that does not serve one or the other, that just is. This truth is the truth nobody wars about. It is the truth that stands on its own. It is the truth that is the very basis of everyone's foundation. It is the truth that is and feels right. It is not made up of stories, serving one against another. This truth is simple. This truth can be felt with your heart. This truth is, simply, the truth.

Sensationalism, nationalism, any "-ism" is not a given prerogative of humanity. The "-isms" exist anywhere in the universe. However, what is unique to humans is your ability to perceive this "-ism" as a given truth, of which there are many. No one truth is solid. There are many probable universes, and there are many truths.

These many truths cannot lead to confusion, as these many probabilities are separated and do not exist within each other.

Seti la. Oti mino toti ku. Seti la seti la. Meni oki na.

This is the end of this communication. Thank you for coming. Namaste and sayonara. Amen.

Remember the Ten Commandments? The Ten Commandments were brought to Moses to correct the ways of human kind. We are bringing the idea of the Ten Commandments to correlate them with the events in Lemuria and Atlantis. The commitment to uphold the Ten Commandments leads to a race that knows its own boundaries, and elevates and betters itself within those boundaries. The race grows within its agreed upon rules without hurting itself and its kind.

The citizens of Lemuria and Atlantis transgressed the established rules and conventions, leading to their downfall and eventual destruction. These transgressions were not necessarily against the Ten Commandments as such, but were against the conduct that confirms humanity's understanding of their own divine origins.

Seti la min su sa and until this day it is said Lemuria is only a dream and that Atlantis has never been.

Is that what you believe? If so, then you need to re-learn that those who live now were involved there. You were in Atlantis and in Lemuria as well. You were in Atlantis and will not heed your own need that is dictating you to unravel that which brought the collapse of that population.

Do you know that you are close to achieving the same fate? Do you know that your fate is coming closer every day? Do you know that your fate is not yet sealed and that the human race can achieve greatness without bringing this world to the brink of disaster?

Oh my sisters, oh my brothers, please be aware of this story. In the end, Atlantis was destroyed in the blink of an eye. Can you imagine the catastrophe? Can you imagine the last hours filled with the horror of knowing that all are sinking into the depths of the ocean called the Atlantic? Do you know that a new Atlantis is already on the rise and that you need to understand what came to pass?

Therefore, listen and be clear. Atlantis' rising is consternation for all, as it shows that not all understand. Be aware that Atlantis can be repeated, and will be, if you do not change your ways of being against your own, of being not one, of being in greed. Be clear that the Atlantis of modern times is rising and you all are responsible for bringing it to a halt. Stop the new Atlantis. Stop it.

The misunderstanding about Atlantis' influence on your culture is evident. We clearly see that you, who lived in Atlantis and are on the planet Earth now, are behaving as people were in those times. You came to change the world, but were caught in the pull of materialistic needs and desires. You forgot that what came to pass in Atlantis is not what you came to bring here. You came here to bring the opposite–the understanding of that which is the spirit and oneness of yourself.

May we clarify that Atlantis' rising refers to the rising of all characteristics that brought the collapse of that culture. May we suggest that you very quickly change your ways, as the obliteration of one third of your world is too drastic of a measure from which to derive the understanding you need to gain.

"Down with greed, down with hatred", needs to be your motto. "Down with the corporate profits without upholding those who are in need". Those who suffer needlessly and are hungry and dying of malnutrition are a shame on this civilization of yours. It shows that you do not care for your brothers and sisters, that you leave them to suffer intolerable conditions, that you amuse yourself while you withhold the support to those who cannot support themselves. We urge you to not allow this to continue. We urge you to not allow Atlantis to rise again.

We urge you to stop intolerance, to stop indulgence, to stop your own prospering on account of those who cannot cover their everyday basics. We urge you to remember that by failing one, you are failing yourself. By not feeding one, you are going hungry on levels you do not yet understand.

We urge you not to swap your souls for goods. We urge you not to swap your integrity for money. We urge you to be aware that Atlantis is rising and will take hold again if you fail to understand that, without change, you will suffer the fate of your ancestors, who are yourselves.

Your awakening is tied to the understanding of your past, and once awakened, you will not repeat your past mistakes in the future. The rising of Atlantis is not what you want to achieve again. You may see Atlantis rising out of the ocean one day. If that happens, you will know that the Earth, in its effort to overturn the decay of humanity, is showing you that the Atlantis at the bottom of the ocean is the Atlantis that you are creating right now.

So take this warning and hold yourself to the principles of a brotherhood and sisterhood of all, as that is what you are. You are brothers and sisters of the race that inhabits the planet Earth. You came with the intent of bringing it into the orbit of the 5th dimensional planets.

Your understanding needs to move from a closed to an open state. With the rising of Atlantis, the Earth, while shedding your wrongdoings, is presenting you with the lost continent of Atlantis in its glory and destruction. It will rise if you do not heed this warning. And once risen, you will have already slid into another, even bigger Atlantis. So listen and be warned. Be ready to stop the rising, as once you understand your past, it will signify the beginning of a new world order on your planet.

And with that, namaste and sayonara. We love you and we cherish you.

Bi li la ti? Eti la kuti? Der ti muli na? Seti oki na? Meti la, meti la.

Be ready to count yourself in and be ready to allow yourself to acquire the patience to unravel this encoding:

"Seti la ait mu. Seti la ai. Deti aki tu. Sa it mulit. Enti la ehti la."

This warning is as current as it can be. We love you and cherish you. Amen.

⁌ ⁍

Sinu mati oka ti. Bu ti me tu anoti. De la ami note be. Me nu ato suirene. De la me ami no. Dela mi ami no. Seti la oti me no. Seti la omi meno.

Those who were killed during the 2nd World War are coming back. Their intent is to redeem themselves in various capacities that lead to peace, not war. Some of them are already here and are chagrined by what is happening at this time. As we speak, there is more and more warmongering going on. There are environmental catastrophes of large proportions occurring. The weather patterns are changing.

During the 2nd World War, groups of people worked together in resistance movements. This is like a resistance movement. We are working together to demonstrate peaceful ways of living on your planet. We are working together to demonstrate that such living is achievable. We are here to make you understand that without resistance to the wrongdoings of your tycoons and those in political and economic power, you cannot achieve the necessary changes. The power of a few together can bring big results.

The movement needs to reach a certain momentum. The movement needs to accumulate enough momentum to break through the barrier of disinterest. The rest of the population needs to be ignited into the realization that the ways employed today are not sustainable for much longer.

Such will be the power that the present systems will topple. The rest is then up to all of you to build that which is peace loving and serving all, not just a few demographically favoured people who have gathered at all reaches of the globe to usurp the planet's natural resources without any consideration for the consequences.

We wish you all the best on your quest toward the changes within and without. That is all for now. Your angels and archangels.

✍ ᢒ

Seti la seti la seti la. Diru mi? Ati ko le mi? Seti la, seti la seti la. A e mone k ti. Ase mone k ti. Dira ma na seti la. Ati mo ki nole tu. Aki mole ti ku. Eti mole seti la. Eti la su limo nme. Eti la ati mone. Ami no k oti la eti mone la. Deri kuli oti ma.

There is a saying that the pupil follows the teacher. The teacher is ready when the pupil is. The pupil is ready when the teacher is. Therefore, you are ready as we are ready. We all are ready and are marching toward the full realization of our given potentials.

This is the last leg of our dictation. Did we get everything? Hmm... what is everything? There is always more. There is so much that you could sit writing day and night until the end of your lives.

This discourse could be one of many, many more, but nevertheless we are finished. We no longer wish to dictate for this book, as it is time to assemble it and take it to the printer. The publisher will materialize. When the book is ready, so will be the publisher. We would like the writer to think the same way, as then the publisher will appear. So Helena, get ready to assemble these dictations and we will soon be ready to start dictating a new book.

Many will read these words. Many will crave their natural state. Many will remember that the most pleasant joys of their lives are simple. Many will come and go, remembering that life in its most precious form is simple. Simplicity is the way of your heart. Clear and simple is your heart. Clear and beautiful are your surroundings if you allow them to be natural.

And with that, we would like to thank all for their participation. We would like to thank you for your dedication. We would like to thank you for your staying power and enthusiasm. May we meet again and continue to bring this fine material to those who are in need of that last little helping nudge toward their own realization of the potential they possess.

We wish you all the best. It has been a pleasure working with you. Bye for now.

About the Author

Helena Kalivoda is a mother of three living in Calgary, Alberta, Canada. She was born in Czechoslovakia, where she studied and received a BA in Economics. In 1968, she immigrated with her husband to Canada and returned to school in 1982 to receive a B.Sc. in Computer Science from the University of Calgary. She was employed as a computer specialist until October 1, 1997, when she retired to compile the writings she began accumulating in the early nineties. Initially, the messages came in verse. Later, once she became comfortable with the thought of receiving such communications, she started writing in prose.

Toward the end of 2001, she became very ill. In her effort to become well again, she fought to understand the origins of her sickness and out of her struggle, the book *AWAKEN!* was born. This book is a collection of messages that she received as answers to her search for the meaning and purpose of her life. Today, the information still flows, as she sits down to record what is transmitted to her every day.